THE WORST
FINANCIAL
MISTAKES
IN THE BIBLE

and
How You Can
Avoid Them

CHUCK BENTLEY

ISBN: 978-1-56427-312-3

Editor: Michael J. Dowling (www.MichaelJDowling.com)
Cover Design: Sean Allen
Interior Art and Design: Sean Allen

THE WORST
FINANCIAL
MISTAKES

IN THE BIBLE

and
How You Can
Avoid Them

CHUCK BENTLEY

God's Wisdom

Heed the Warnings And Enjoy the Blessings

Since they hated knowledge
and did not choose to fear the Lord,

since they would not accept my advice
and spurned my rebuke,

they will eat the fruit of their ways
and be filled with the fruit of their schemes.

For the waywardness of the simple will kill them,
and the complacency of fools will destroy them;

but whoever listens to me will live in safety
and be at ease, without fear of harm.

Proverbs 1:29-33

Acknowledgements

Ann Wagner Bentley

You once asked me how I thought I was going to be the CEO of a global ministry, a husband, a dad and still manage to find the time to write another book. Well…now you know! *You* are the secret ingredient to making it all happen.

Thank you, Ann, for all the ways you serve our family and me yet still manage to shape and edit my manuscripts. May you derive eternal joy by how God chooses to use this book.

Dr. Paul Shin
Nan Hee Park

Your encouragement to share this message more broadly when I delivered my talk at the Asia Pacific Reunion in Thailand caused me to seriously consider writing the book. Thank you and the Crown Korea team for all of your hard work and support.

Heather Hayes
Shelia Thompson

You insisted on getting this book into print. Thank you for believing in this project and working so hard to make it possible.

Sean Allen

Your keen talent to give a book its personality and enhance its likelihood of being read is a real blessing to the reader. May you receive due credit for your artistic enhancements of this entire project.

Michael J. Dowling

Thank you for the professional editing and technical input on the manuscript. You are a joy to work with. I hope other writers will seek your services and godly advice.

Chuck Thompson

Thank you for helping me to research the topic and provide valuable insight. You encouraged me at time when the deadline looked impossible to meet.

ontents

Introduction

ost of us tend to identify more with the heroes and heroines of the Bible than with the characters who made the big mistakes. For example, we naturally gravitate to David more than to Saul, to Sarah more than to Hagar, and certainly to the Apostle John more than to the disciple Judas. Personally, I much prefer to read about Peter's boldness on the day of Pentecost than about his humiliating denial of Christ before the crucifixion.

But mistakes, failures, and defeats are a part of the normal human experience. We can learn many valuable lessons from studying the mistakes of others and from looking honestly at our own. As Christians, we can revisit our failures without fear or shame, because "we know that in all things God works for the good of those who love him, who have been called according to his purpose." (Romans 8:28)

For many years I've enjoyed the privilege of teaching others about biblical financial principles and practices. I realized recently, however, that I've seldom considered the mistakes made by people in the Bible. That itself is a mistake, because we often can learn as much or more from failures as from successes.

This is certainly true when it comes to understanding God's financial principles. In Proverbs, the positive example of the frugal saver and the negative example of the poverty-stricken sluggard are both valuable for gaining wisdom.

In these pages, I highlight my list of the worst financial mistakes recorded in the Bible. They're presented chronologically so they correlate with the referenced Biblical passages. The Bible identifies many more financial mistakes than I have addressed, and I encourage you to look for them and learn from them.

When I started doing research for this book, I expected to find that most financial mistakes in the Bible were due to poor money-management practices. But I was surprised to see how few stories revolved around the improper handling of debt, savings, investing, planning for the future, and other such topics. The primary culprit was not wrong practices but wrong priorities.

The people of the Bible who made the biggest financial mistakes had the wrong heart attitudes and the wrong motives. Their problems started when they abandoned the Word of God and bought into the "wisdom" of the world.

The best way to avoid the financial mistakes chronicled in these pages is to undergo a radical transformation of your beliefs about money. I'm talking about a complete change of heart! Those who want to reap the eternal dividends God promises to the faithful must follow the advice the Apostle Paul gives in Romans 12:2:

> *Do not conform to the pattern of this world, but be transformed by the renewing of your mind. Then you will be able to test and approve what God's will is—his good, pleasing and perfect will.*

To get the most from this book, I suggest that you read only one chapter per day or per week. Take time to meditate on the truths God has for you. Begin each session with prayer, asking the Holy Spirit to reveal the wisdom of the lesson. Next, read the entire Biblical passage referenced at the beginning of each chapter. Finally, read the lesson and complete the practical application.

The lessons are designed to stimulate rich conversations about some of the most common financial mistakes and how to avoid them. They are an excellent resource for small-group discussion.

I pray that God will powerfully use this book in your life to redeem your past financial mistakes and conform your future financial decisions to his good, pleasing and perfect will.

Chuck Bentley
June 2013

chapter 1

Seeking the Best the World Has to Offer

Surrender Our Desires
to Always Have the Best

GENESIS 13:1-13

rom the very beginning, Satan has tempted man with the desire to have the best the world has to offer. Selfish pride in our possessions is a common financial mistake. Like every issue with pride, it is easy to recognize in others, but very hard to see in ourselves.

We can learn a great deal from the story of Abram's nephew, Lot, who foolishly chose for himself the best the world had to offer. Genesis 13:1-9 tells us that Abram and Lot went up together to a place between Bethel and Ai, but the land would not support all of their flocks, herds, and tents, so quarreling arose between their herders.

Abram, who was about seventy-five years old at the time, had the wisdom to recognize that these quarrels would damage his relationship with his nephew, whom he loved. Both men were already very wealthy, but only Abram valued their relationship more than money. To end their conflict, Abram graciously allowed Lot to choose which land he preferred.

THE CHOICE

Lot looked around and saw that the whole plain of the Jordan toward Zoar was well watered, like the garden of the Lord, like the land of Egypt. (This was before the Lord destroyed Sodom and Gomorrah.) So Lot chose for himself the whole plain of the Jordan and set out toward the east. The two men parted company: Abram lived in the land of Canaan, while Lot lived among the cities of the plain and pitched his tents near Sodom. Now the people of Sodom were wicked and were sinning greatly against the Lord.

(Genesis 13:10-13)

Thinking only of himself and his flocks, Lot chose the "well-watered" land. That may have been a wise economic choice from a worldly standpoint, because flocks will die without water, but it was an unwise and selfish choice in God's economy. Lot not only failed to respect his uncle, who was his elder, but he ignored the risks of living close to Sodom, which the Bible describes as a population of "wicked people—those sinning greatly against the Lord."

THE CONSEQUENCES

This decision had disastrous results for Lot. As we learn in Genesis 14, Sodom and Gomorrah are later invaded; King Kedorlaomer and a contingent of other kings seize Lot and all of his possessions. Lot is now a captive who ultimately must be rescued by his Uncle Abram. In Genesis 19, we read that Lot must be rescued again, this time by angels as Sodom is being destroyed, and his wife loses her life in the process.

Abram, on the other hand, was blessed by God:

> *The Lord said to Abram after Lot had parted from him, "Look around from where you are, to the north and south, to the east and west. All the land that you see I will give to you and your offspring forever. I will make your offspring like the dust of the earth, so that if anyone could count the dust, then your offspring could be counted. Go, walk through the length and breadth of the land, for I am giving it to you."*
>
> (Genesis 13:14-17)

Lot chose independently of God to possess the best land, but in a very short time he lost it. Abram honored God by giving up the best land, and God ultimately returned all the land to him as an eternal possession.

CHOOSING THE BEST FOR OURSELVES

We naturally want the best for ourselves, and marketers around the world know how to exploit this common human tendency. They use phrases like "you deserve the best" to help us justify our carnal appetites. They push the benefits of more, bigger, better, or faster in advertisements to create discontent with our present possessions or circumstances. A Dallas businessman who worked very hard to climb the social status ladder was fond of saying, "I was born desiring the 'deluxe package' for my life." Aren't we all!

Young North Korean leader Kim Jung Un is responsible for the misery and suffering of 22 million people. Most citizens in his country have barely enough food to survive; yet he draws on an estimated personal net worth of more than $5 billion dollars to feed his voracious appetite for luxuries. As an example of his extravagance, he flew his favorite retired NBA star to his country from the United States, simply to gratify his fanatic love of basketball. He apparently learned the art of self-gratification from his late father, who reportedly added $800,000 worth of the world's best liquor every year to his personal stockpile.

How to Avoid the Trap of Prideful Selfishness

When we see others choosing the best for themselves, we are quick to label them as selfish. But it's much more difficult to notice this same tendency in ourselves. What lessons can we learn from scripture that will help us avoid Lot's fatal mistake?

- First, we can follow the advice of the Apostle Paul in Philippians 2:3-4:

> *Do nothing out of selfish ambition or vain conceit.*
> *Rather, in humility value others above yourselves, not*
> *looking to your own interests but each of you to the*
> *interests of the others.*

Abram displayed this type of generosity toward Lot when he surrendered his rights to the best land. He did so again when he risked his life to fight for his nephew's freedom. We know from the book of Acts that this generous attitude was a hallmark of the early Church.

- Second, we can remember that we are surrounded by a great cloud of witnesses who over the centuries have been willing to accept the loss of earthly possessions for the sake of enduring gain.

You suffered along with those in prison and joyfully accepted the confiscation of your property, because you knew that you yourselves had better and lasting possessions. So do not throw away your confidence; it will be richly rewarded.

(Hebrews 10:34-35)

We possess a faith this is "much more precious than gold." (1 Peter 1:7) Even though this invaluable spiritual possession is unseen, we have confidence that it is real and lasting.

Having the best is not wrong. In fact, scripture tells us in Proverbs 24:3-4, *"By wisdom a house is built, and through understanding it is established; through knowledge its rooms are filled with rare and beautiful treasures."* The problem arises when we want the best for ourselves for selfish reasons. Ultimately, it's an issue of the motives of our heart, not simply a matter of possessions.

Jesus admonishes us to be willing to give up earthly gratification for heavenly rewards in Luke 14:8-11:

When someone invites you to a wedding feast, do not take the place of honor, for a person more distinguished than you may have been invited. If so, the host who invited both of you will come and say to you, "Give this person your seat." Then, humiliated, you will have to take the least important place. But when you are invited, take the lowest place, so that when your host comes, he will say to you, "Friend, move up to a better place." Then you will be honored in the presence of all the other guests. For all those who exalt themselves will be humbled, and those who humble themselves will be exalted.

Our natural desire is to want possessions, honor, and other things for our glory or security or pleasure. God wants us to put our love for him first and trust him to provide us what we need.

As long as we are in this world, we will be tempted to gratify our worldly appetites by means of selfish financial choices. To overcome these temptations, we must:

- Learn to identify the places where we are most vulnerable

- Surrender our desire to always have the best.

- Ask others we trust to help hold us accountable

- Wait 30 days before making a major purchase to thwart the desire for instant gratification

- Quickly repent of jealousy when others obtain what we would like to have

- Nurture our devotion to God, so that our knowledge of his love and our confidence in his promises fully satisfy all of our longings.

If we practice these principles, we will reap daily contentment and an eternal inheritance. A graphic portrayal of these truths is found in the short film "Abram's Reward," part of the *God Provides*® series, available from Crown (www.crown.org).

chapter 2

Hidden Greed

Contentment is the Only
Antidote to Desiring More

NUMBERS 22:21-32

ore than likely, you have heard the colorful story of Balaam, the man of God who was rebuked by a donkey. When he was approached by Moabite officials offering to pay him a large amount of money for cursing the children of Israel, he declined to go with them after consulting with God. Balak, the king of the Moabites, sent more important messengers with an even larger "diviners fee," and this time Balaam agreed to go. Although he insisted that he would not curse the children of Israel, his actions indicated that he hoped to somehow obtain that rich financial reward. We pick up the story in Numbers 22:21:

THE CHOICE

Balaam got up in the morning, saddled his donkey and went with the Moabite officials. But God was very angry when he went, and the angel of the Lord stood in the road to oppose him. Balaam was riding on his donkey, and his two servants were with him. When the donkey saw the angel of the Lord standing in the road with a drawn sword in his hand, it turned off the road into a field. Balaam beat it to get it back on the road.

Then the angel of the Lord stood in a narrow path through the vineyards, with walls on both sides. When the donkey saw the angel of the Lord, it pressed close to the wall, crushing Balaam's foot against it. So he beat the donkey again.

Then the angel of the Lord moved on ahead and stood in a narrow place where there was no room to turn, either to the right or to the left. When the donkey saw the angel of the Lord, it lay down under Balaam, and he was angry and beat it with his staff. Then the Lord opened the donkey's mouth, and it said to Balaam, "What have I done to you to make you beat me these three times?"

Balaam answered the donkey, "You have made a fool of me! If only I had a sword in my hand, I would kill you right now."

The donkey said to Balaam, "Am I not your own donkey, which you have always ridden, to this day? Have I been in the habit of doing this to you?"

"No," he said.

Then the Lord opened Balaam's eyes, and he saw the angel of the Lord standing in the road with his sword drawn. So he bowed low and fell facedown.

The angel of the Lord asked him, "Why have you beaten your donkey these three times? I have come here to oppose you because your path is a reckless one before me."

Balaam was tempted by the prospect of large personal financial gain. An angel of the Lord was prepared to strike him down, but God used a humble donkey to mercifully spare him. Lessons from Balaam's bad example are referred to in Deuteronomy, Joshua, Nehemiah, Micah, 2 Peter, Jude, and Revelation. This was a story to be remembered!

WHY IS GREED BAD?

In an interview at Columbia University, New York City pastor Dr. Tim Keller expressed a key insight when it comes to hidden greed:

"Jesus talks about greed ten times more than he talks about adultery. You know when you are committing adultery, but almost no one knows that they are greedy. We are always comparing ourselves to other people....it's a frog-in-the-kettle kind of thing. However, the fact of the matter is that the Bible is much harder on greed than on materialism. It's a horrible sin, a terrible sin."

Like most people, I have difficulty appreciating how offensive greed is to God. I tend to think that if the weight of greed were on one side of the scale, and weight of adultery was on the other, the scales would tip towards adultery as the heavier, more consequential sin. But this is not God's view.

God abhors greed. Perhaps more than any other sin, greed reveals what we think about him. Greed indicates that we are placing a higher priority on things than on our relationship with God. Our thoughts and actions reveal our priorities and loyalties. We are guilty of gross sin when our desire to acquire more money and possessions is greater than our desire to love and obey God.

THE CONSEQUENCES

If you take a quick survey of all the places in the Bible where greed was identified and punished by God, the findings will shock you. God's punishment for greed can be described as severe. Ananias and Sapphira fell dead when their hidden greed was discovered. This event sent "great fear" throughout the entire Church, as recorded in Acts 5. God is serious about the purity of his Church. More about these two later.

Balaam himself came to a terrible demise. He was killed by the sword as God had Israel take revenge on the Midianites. Numbers 31 records that even the followers of Balaam's advice were punished for their sin of unfaithfulness:

> *They were the ones who followed Balaam's advice and*
> *enticed the Israelites to be unfaithful to the Lord in the Peor*
> *incident, so that a plague struck the Lord's people.*

Paul gave the following stern warning of the consequences of greed and its devastating effect upon our commitment to the Lord in 1 Timothy 6:9-10:

> *Those who want to get rich fall into temptation and a trap*
> *and into many foolish and harmful desires that plunge*
> *people into ruin and destruction. For the love of money is a*

*root of all kinds of evil. Some people, eager for money, have
wandered from the faith and pierced themselves with
many griefs.*

Hidden greed can lead to a) traps, b) foolish and self-destructive desires, c) ruin and destruction, and d) wandering from the faith. These are described as "many griefs" brought about by self-inflicted wounds.

How to Avoid the Trap of Hidden Greed

Contentment is the only true antidote to greed.

*Keep your lives free from the love of money and be content
with what you have, because God has said, "Never will I
leave you; never will I forsake you."*
(Hebrews 13:5)

Contentment means the joyful acceptance that God is sufficient to meet all of our needs for today. But contentment must be learned through practice. Paul said that we can learn to be content whether we have a lot or a little, but it requires a change of heart and mind.

Colossians 3:1-3 makes it clear that greed must be stopped in the privacy of our own thoughts and desires:

*Since, then, you have been raised with Christ, set your
hearts on things above, where Christ is, seated at the
right hand of God. Set your minds on things above,
not on earthly things. For you died, and your life is
now hidden with Christ in God.*

Professional marketers get paid big bucks to make us discontent by using extraordinarily sophisticated techniques to get us to desire what we don't have. They want us to fix our eyes on temporal things, but God wants us to fix our eyes on Jesus.

We need to renew our mind with God's truth and set our heart on things that have eternal value. Our deepest needs can never be met with more things; they can only be satisfied with more of Jesus.

chapter

APPLICATION

When faced with a financial choice, follow these three simple steps to avoid falling into the trap of hidden greed:

- Ask yourself if your desire is for a real need. If not, ask yourself if you can live without it.

- Pray and ask God for clarity about your decision. Seek counsel from others regarding your motives and intentions, and make yourself accountable to their wisdom.

- If you are confident that your contentment in Christ will not be altered, with or without the purchase, proceed in peace with whatever you want to do.

chapter

Embezzling God's Property

Recognize that God Owns Everything

Joshua 7

mbezzlement is the fraudulent conversion of another's property by a person who is in a position of trust, such as an agent or employee. Most nations treat embezzlement as a serious crime, punishable by significant penalties in both civil and criminal courts.

In Joshua 7, we read how Achan stole God's property and claimed it as his own. He may be the first man in the Bible who attempted to embezzle from God. If embezzlement from other people is a serious crime, how much more serious is embezzlement from God!

The story of his brazen theft and the lessons it teaches are known as the "Sin of Achan." To fully understand the seriousness of Achan's sin, we must understand the circumstances surrounding it. The nation of Israel had sought God's help to overcome the heavily fortified city of Jericho. The Lord gave the army an unconventional means to bring down this daunting foe, with the stipulation that they devote all of the spoils of victory exclusively to his honor.

Under the leadership of Joshua, the Israelites followed God's instructions. The walls of Jericho came crashing down and the city was captured, without the loss of one Israelite soldier. The victors collected the large amount of spoils and "devoted" them to God. As used here, the Hebrew term for "devoted" means "an irrevocable giving over of things or persons to the Lord, often by totally destroying them."

It's not clear why God told the Israelites to set apart the spoils of battle for him, but I have an idea. I think He wanted to discourage them from becoming a conquering militia bent on acquiring wealth through warfare. So, He withheld the "things" and gave them the land, in fulfillment of the promise he had given to Abraham.

Following the victory at Jericho, the Israelites went out to battle against the people of Ai. They were routed, losing thirty-six men in the process. Joshua was stunned! Why had God's people suffered this defeat? He fell before the Lord and asked for an explanation. In Joshua 7:10-15, we read God's answer:

> *The LORD said to Joshua, "Stand up! What are you doing*
> *down on your face? Israel has sinned; they have violated my*

covenant, which I commanded them to keep. They have taken some of the devoted things; they have stolen, they have lied, they have put them with their own possessions. That is why the Israelites cannot stand against their enemies; they turn their backs and run because they have been made liable to destruction. I will not be with you anymore unless you destroy whatever among you is devoted to destruction.

"Go, consecrate the people. Tell them, 'Consecrate yourselves in preparation for tomorrow; for this is what the LORD, the God of Israel, says: There are devoted things among you, Israel. You cannot stand against your enemies until you remove them.

"'In the morning, present yourselves tribe by tribe. The tribe the LORD chooses shall come forward clan by clan; the clan the LORD chooses shall come forward family by family; and the family the LORD chooses shall come forward man by man. Whoever is caught with the devoted things shall be destroyed by fire, along with all that belongs to him. He has violated the covenant of the LORD and has done an outrageous thing in Israel!'"

Notice that the Lord describes this sin as "outrageous." It is not a trivial financial mistake, as we shall soon discover.

THE REST OF THE STORY

Joshua 7:16-18 tells us how God identified the guilty person:

Early the next morning Joshua had Israel come forward by tribes, and Judah was chosen. The clans of Judah came forward, and the Zerahites were chosen. He had the clan of the Zerahites come forward by families, and Zimri was

*chosen. Joshua had his family come forward man by man,
and Achan son of Karmi, the son of Zimri, the son of Zerah,
of the tribe of Judah, was chosen.*

Imagine how Achan's heart must have been pounding as the focus quickly narrowed to the tribe of Judah, then to the clan of the Zerahites, then to the family of Zadi, and finally to Achan. He stood accused before the entire assembly with nowhere to hide.

*Then Joshua said to Achan, "My son, give glory to the
LORD, the God of Israel, and honor him. Tell me what you
have done; do not hide it from me."*

Even though he knew he would receive a severe penalty for his sin, Achan confessed the truth in order to give glory and honor to God:

*Achan replied, "It is true! I have sinned against the LORD,
the God of Israel. This is what I have done: When I saw in
the plunder a beautiful robe from Babylonia, two hundred
shekels of silver and a bar of gold weighing fifty shekels, I
coveted them and took them. They are hidden in the ground
inside my tent, with the silver underneath."*

Take a long look at the list of the "things" that brought Achan down. Note his honest description about how the sin occurred. First he "saw"; then he "coveted"; then he "took"; and finally he "hid." This is the journey to embezzlement.

CONTEMPORARY EMBEZZLERS

Few of us would go into a temple or church and steal the tithes and offerings that worshippers had donated. That would be embezzling from God! But John Piper frequently points out in his sermons that all Christians, without realizing it, are guilty of embezzling God's property.

God does not own the first 10 percent of all the *money we earn*; he owns 100 percent of *everything we have*. Psalm 24:1 spells it out clearly: "*The earth is the Lord's and everything in it, the world and all who live in it.*"

When I describe money and possessions as "mine," I am operating as if I gained all that I have by my own hands. Even worse, I am in effect stating the God has no jurisdiction over my monetary decisions. This attitude is contrary to God's Word. The Bible makes it clear that *"every good and perfect gift is from above."* (James 1:17) We are temporary trustees of all that God has provided to us. This distinction has both temporal and eternal consequences.

In the Texas town where I grew up, the case of the high-profile rancher who claimed to be an heir of the famed Spindletop oil fortune became legendary. Even though this rancher was illiterate and had to sign his name with an X, he lived a luxurious lifestyle complete with corporate jets and lavish parties at his home. Many people "invested" millions of dollars into the "business opportunities" he offered, all of which turned out to be fraudulent.

A friend of mine who actually knew this man told me that an invitation to one of his ultra-expensive parties was once a status symbol. He had deceived even the most educated and successful in the community. However, after he was exposed as a complete swindler, no one wanted to be known as having anything to do with him. It became a badge of honor to NOT have attended one of his parties.

In a similar way, we must be careful not to fall for the deception of the "Great Swindler." Satan wants us to think that we are the owners of the world's wealth, when in fact we are only the temporary trustees. Those who fall for this deception of the enemy will one day want to distance themselves from ever having identified with him or taken part in his lavish parties.

CONSEQUENCES

Witnessing a public execution is a painful experience, but for good reason the Bible records in detail how Achan and his family paid the ultimate price for their sin. The reason is that God wanted future generations to remember this story, so they would not make the same mistake.

So Joshua sent messengers, and they ran to the tent, and there it was, hidden in his tent, with the silver underneath. They took the things from the tent, brought them to Joshua and all the Israelites and spread them out before the LORD.

Then Joshua, together with all Israel, took Achan son of Zerah, the silver, the robe, the gold bar, his sons and daughters, his cattle, donkeys and sheep, his tent and all that he had, to the Valley of Achor.

Joshua said, "Why have you brought this trouble on us? The LORD will bring trouble on you today." Then all Israel stoned him, and after they had stoned the rest, they burned them. Over Achan they heaped up a large pile of rocks, which remains to this day. Then the LORD turned from his fierce anger. Therefore that place has been called the Valley of Achor ever since.

(Joshua 7:22-26)

Achan's embezzlement of the things devoted to God was a costly mistake. His personal disobedience cost the lives of thirty-six Israelites. It then cost him his life and the life of his entire family, along with all their possessions. They were stoned, burned, and buried under a heap of stones in the Valley of Achor. Unforgettable! God is serious about this financial mistake.

How to Avoid the Trap of Embezzlement

To resist the ever-present temptation to claim God's possessions as our own, we must become vigilant and strong. We must first acknowledge that God truly does own everything we have. Next, we must commit to faithfully use them as a steward or temporary trustee. Finally, we must liberally give God's possessions for God's purposes.

In 1 Chronicles 29:11-12, David provides a great example of acknowledging God's ownership of all things in his prayer following the receiving of gifts for the building of the temple of the Lord:

> *Everything in the heavens and earth is yours, O Lord, and this is your kingdom. We adore you as being in control of everything. Riches and honor come from you alone, and you are the Ruler of all mankind; your hand controls power and might, and it is at your discretion that men are made great and given strength.* (TLB)

chapter

APPLICATION

- Make a list of everything that God has entrusted to you: money, stocks, bonds, land, home, vehicles, gold, real estate, and whatever else is currently under your control.

- Create a document called "God's Possessions Temporarily Entrusted to My Care." Put everything in the first list on this document.

- Determine how to best use these resources to bring glory to God and advance his kingdom.

- Meditate upon 1 Chronicles 29:11-12.

chapter 4

Refusing to Help When Help Is Needed

Seize Opportunities to Share at All Times

1 SAMUEL 25

eet Nabal, a man whose name can be translated to mean "senseless fool." Although he is a very rich man, owning three thousand sheep and one thousand goats, his demeanor is described in 1 Samuel 25 as "surly and mean."

In this passage, we learn that David and about 600 of his followers were hiding from King Saul in the vicinity of Carmel, where Nabal's men happened to be sheering his huge flock of sheep. It would have been easy for David and his men to take some of Nabal's sheep to supply their needs for food and wool. But instead, they provided protection for Nabal's sheep and shearers, asking nothing in return.

Finally, David sent ten of his men to politely ask Nabal for a minimal amount of food and other resources. Nabal was already very wealthy, and he was about to gain even more wealth from the wool he would soon sell. One would think he would be in a generous and joyous mood, but he was not. Here was his answer:

> *Then Nabal answered David's servants, and said, "Who is this David? Who is this son of Jesse? Many servants are breaking away from their masters these days. Why should I take my bread and water, and the meat I have slaughtered for my shearers, and give it to men coming from who knows where?"*
>
> (1 Samuel 25:10-11)

Nabal has no obvious justification for hoarding his vast wealth and refusing David's reasonable request for help. Going even beyond stinginess and pride, he actually took advantage of David's distressed condition. Instead of helping, he insulted David, questioned his motives, and bluntly asserted that he had no interest in sharing anything. No wonder he was called arrogant, churlish, and mean!

At this time, David was in desperate need, but soon he would become king. What an opportunity Nabal missed! Later he paid a terrible price.

Nabal's beautiful and gracious wife, Abigail, whose name refers to "rejoicing at God's work or attributes," responded completely differently. When she found out about her husband's selfish actions, she interceded in an attempt to prevent David from killing him. After supplying David and his men food and wine, she appealed to David with the following words:

> *…Pardon your servant, my lord, and let me speak to you; hear what your servant has to say. Please pay no attention, my lord, to that wicked man Nabal. He is just like his name—his name means Fool, and folly goes with him. And as for me, your servant, I did not see the men my lord sent.*
>
> *And now, my lord, as surely as the Lord your God lives and as you live, since the Lord has kept you from bloodshed and from avenging yourself with your own hands, may your enemies and all who are intent on harming my lord be like Nabal. And let this gift, which your servant has brought to my lord, be given to the men who follow you.*
>
> *Please forgive your servant's presumption. The Lord your God will certainly make a lasting dynasty for my lord, because you fight the Lord's battles, and no wrongdoing will be found in you as long as you live. Even though someone is pursuing you to take your life, the life of my lord will be bound securely in the bundle of the living by the Lord your God, but the lives of your enemies he will hurl away as from the pocket of a sling. When the Lord has fulfilled for my lord every good thing he promised concerning him and has appointed him ruler over Israel, my lord will not have on his conscience the staggering burden of needless bloodshed or of having avenged himself. And when the Lord your God has brought my lord success, remember your servant.*

(1 Samuel 25:24-31)

SHARING AND SIGNIFICANCE

In the world's economy, significance is gained through the ownership and possession of assets. In God's economy, significance is gained through sharing of our assets. Far too many people make the big mistake of hoarding money instead of giving it away. They refuse to respond to the needs of others, even when these opportunities are quite obviously presented by God.

Paradoxically, research indicates that lower-income people are more willing to share than people with considerable means. In the United States, low-income earners donate almost three times more as a percentage of income than high-income earners. The New Testament points to the poor as the greatest givers. Jesus commended the widow who gave all she had (Luke 21:3-4), and the Apostle Paul praised the Macedonians, who gave out of their extreme poverty (2 Corinthians 8:2). May these and other examples of sharing inspire us to greater generosity.

Guatemala City, Guatemala, is home to one of the largest church buildings in the world. When I had the privilege of visiting this massive, state-of-the-art facility, I was shocked to learn from the pastor that the congregation consists of lower-income families. I asked him, "How did you get the money to build such an incredible structure, while so many churches in the world struggle with a lack of funding?"

He said, "All of us as Christians derive our meaning and purpose in life from our salvation, from our relationship with Jesus Christ. But we derive our significance on earth from sharing whatever we have. Acts 20:35 says, 'It is more blessed to give than to receive.' Our congregation wants to be significant, and sharing with others is God's way out of poverty of the soul." What a profound response!

CONSEQUENCES

Nabal's foolish desire to keep everything he owned led to his utter destruction. The rest of the story is a fascinating look into the immediate reversal of fortune that came upon this wealthy, yet self-absorbed man.

While Nabal was feasting like a "king" and celebrating in high spirits and drunkenness at his luxurious banquet, the future king David and his men were suffering. On the morning following his banquet, Nabal learned from Abigail that she had helped David and his followers. This shocking news sent Nabal into cardiac arrest, literally! The Bible records that *"his heart died within him, and he became like a stone. Then it happened, after about ten days, the Lord struck Nabal and he died."* (1 Samuel 25:37-38)

Proverbs 11:26 says, *"People curse the one who hoards grain, but they pray God's blessing on the one who is willing to sell."* God did indeed bless Abigail. She became the wife of King David.

How to Avoid the Trap of Stinginess

God presents all of us with opportunities to share with others. Will we respond like Nabal or Abigail? We can guard our hearts and minds against stinginess by meditating on and abiding by scriptures like the following:

> *Therefore, as we have opportunity, let us do good to all people, especially to those who belong to the family of believers.*
>
> (Galatians 6:10)

> *Be wise in the way you act toward outsiders; make the most of every opportunity.*
>
> (Colossians 4:5)

> *Remember this: Whoever sows sparingly will also reap sparingly, and whoever sows generously will also reap generously. Each of you should give what you have decided in your heart to give, not reluctantly or under compulsion, for God loves a cheerful giver.*
>
> (2 Corinthians 9:6-7)

My wife and I try to keep our eyes and hearts open so we will not miss opportunities to experience the joy of sharing. Outside of our normal planned giving, I carry an amount of cash in my wallet so we will be prepared when we encounter people in need. Some of my most satisfying acts of generosity have come from responding to these unexpected opportunities.

APPLICATION

To apply the principles presented in this lesson, take an inventory of your attitudes about sharing. The following questions may stimulate your thinking:

- If you were to create a graph about sharing by putting Abigail at the top and Nabal at the bottom, where would you place yourself?

- How do you respond when you see needs? For example, when you see a charity soliciting funds as you enter a store, do you think of this encounter as an opportunity or a nuisance?

- Have you experienced the joy of spontaneously meeting someone else's need? If so, how did it feel?

- Have you ever refused to meet a need and later regretted it?

- Are you aware of any immediate needs that God may be presenting to you?

chapter 5

Coveting What Others Have

Coveting Is Conquered Only by Loving Our Neighbor

1 KINGS 21

 ver met anyone named Ahab or Jezebel? Neither have I. They effectively destroyed those names for all future generations by their outrageous standard of wickedness. While it is easy to dismiss them as having no redeeming qualities, we can actually learn much from their mistakes. As my father taught me, we are always an example, but the choice is whether we are a good one or bad one.

King Ahab spotted a beautiful garden in a prime location close to his palace. For generations it had been in the family of a man named Naboth, and it was not for sale. That did not deter Ahab from coveting what was not legally or morally his. He made an offer to buy the garden, which Naboth flatly turned down. Even though the value of the plot of land was trivial in view of Ahab's possessions, the king sunk into a sullen state of misery.

Enter Queen Jezebel to save the day. No lowly gardener should deny the king the desires of his heart, she told him. She devised a wicked plan, detailed in 1 Kings 21, which led to the cruel stoning death of Naboth. Thus, she acquired the garden and satisfied her frustrated husband. The Bible comments on this act:

> *There was never anyone like Ahab, who sold himself to do evil in the eyes of the Lord, urged on by Jezebel his wife. He behaved in the vilest manner by going after idols....*(v. 25-26)

One of Ahab's many idols was to have a vegetable garden near his residence.

THE TENTH COMMANDMENT

God prohibited coveting in the tenth commandment, but I know of no culture that has ever attempted to outlaw this sin. Only God can hold us accountable for this destructive heart attitude.

Coveting differs slightly from greed. Greed is desiring what we do not have (or don't have enough of). Coveting is desiring what *others* have. It is based on comparisons and rooted in pride. As C. S. Lewis so aptly said, "Pride gets no pleasure out of having something, only out of having more of it than the next man."

CONSEQUENCES

Ahab and Jezebel likely believed that their sin would bring no consequences. Naboth was dead, the garden was in their possession, and Ahab was able to have his vegetables. But read carefully the judgment God delivered to Ahab through his servant Elijah:

> *Then the word of the Lord came to Elijah the Tishbite: "Go down to meet Ahab king of Israel, who rules in Samaria. He is now in Naboth's vineyard, where he has gone to take possession of it. Say to him, 'This is what the Lord says: Have you not murdered a man and seized his property?' Then say to him, 'This is what the Lord says: In the place where dogs licked up Naboth's blood, dogs will lick up your blood—yes, yours!'"*
>
> *Ahab said to Elijah, "So you have found me, my enemy!"*
>
> *"I have found you," he answered, "because you have sold yourself to do evil in the eyes of the Lord. He says, 'I am going to bring disaster on you. I will wipe out your descendants and cut off from Ahab every last male in Israel—slave or free. I will make your house like that of Jeroboam son of Nebat and that of Baasha son of Ahijah, because you have aroused my anger and have caused Israel to sin.'*
>
> *"And also concerning Jezebel the Lord says: 'Dogs will devour Jezebel by the wall of Jezreel.' Dogs will eat those belonging to Ahab who die in the city, and the birds will feed on those who die in the country."*
>
> (1 Kings 21:17-24)

Ahab was shaken to his core and repented of this sin. Nevertheless, the Bible records in 2 Kings 9 that the words of Elijah were fulfilled. Dogs devoured Jezebel at the very location prophesied by Elijah.

The Bible severely warns us of the consequences of coveting:

> *For of this you can be sure: No immoral, impure, or greedy*
> *person—such a person is an idolater—has any inheritance*
> *in the kingdom of Christ and of God. Let no one deceive you*
> *with empty words, for because of such things God's wrath*
> *comes on those who are disobedient.*
>
> (Ephesians 5:5-6)

When we harbor prideful desires for what others have, our hearts turn cold toward God. He is no longer the treasure that satisfies our needs. In his classic work, *The Pursuit of God,* A. W. Tozer says the following about the issue of pride of ownership:

> "Our woes began when God was forced out of His central shrine and things were allowed to enter. Within the human heart things have taken over. Men have now by nature no peace within their hearts, for God is crowned there no longer, but there in the moral dusk, stubborn and aggressive usurpers fight amongst themselves for first place on the throne.

> "This is not a mere metaphor, but an accurate analysis of our real spiritual trouble. There is within the human heart a tough, fibrous root of fallen life whose nature is to possess, always to possess. It covets things with a deep and fierce passion.

> "The pronouns *my* and *mine* look innocent enough in print, but their constant and universal use is significant. They express the real nature of the old Adamic man better than a thousand volumes of theology do. They are verbal symptoms of our deep disease. The roots of our heart have grown down deep into things, and we dare not pull up one rootlet lest we die. Things have become necessary to us, a development never originally intended. God's gifts now take the place of God, and the whole course of nature is upset by the monstrous substitution."

How to Avoid the Trap of Covetousness

Paul spoke openly about how he wrestled with the temptation to covet. God used this issue, among others, to show him the power of the law to condemn, and the riches of his grace to deliver us to freedom from death. Romans 13:9 reveals the antidote Paul found for this temptation:

> *The commandments, "Do not commit adultery," "Do not murder," "Do not steal," "Do not covet," and whatever other commandment there may be, are summed up in this one rule: "Love your neighbor as yourself."*

God's royal law is to love others as much as we love ourselves. This means we can rejoice over what God has provided for us, and we can rejoice over what God has provided for others. This is the only real solution to the problem of coveting.

APPLICATION

Whenever you identify the spirit of coveting in your heart, take these actions:

- Thank God for what he has provided for you. Thank him for the riches of his mercy in not giving you what you do deserve, and for his grace in giving you what you don't deserve. Thank him for his faithfulness and for his word. Thank him for everything he has done for you. Keep a journal to record your gratitude.

- Thank God for his kindness in providing for others. Rejoice in the goodness and generous blessings he has bestowed on them.

- Pray and ask God to reveal more of his true riches to you, which are far more satisfying than the things of this world.

Excessive Debt

Avoid the Use of Debt

2 Kings 4:1-7

 he Bible frequently doesn't mention the specific names of people who have made really terrible mistakes. Perhaps God gives us these nameless bad examples so we can mentally insert our own name. When we identify with the pain and humiliation of those who have made bad choices, we'll be less likely to commit the same errors.

In 2 Kings 4:1-7, we read about one such big mistake made by a nameless individual. The story begins with this heart-wrenching sentence:

> *The wife of a man from the company of the prophets cried out to Elisha, "Your servant my husband is dead, and you know that he revered the Lord. But now his creditor is coming to take my two boys as his slaves."*

The main culprit is not the widow, nor her children, nor the unmerciful debt collectors. The person responsible for this horrible situation is actually the woman's deceased husband.

Every mother will regard this scenario as a living nightmare. Here we have a vulnerable, helpless widow who has no money and two children to care for. As she struggles to survive, the debt collectors are outside the door demanding her children as payment for the debts of her late husband. Proverbs 22:7 says that the "borrower is servant to the lender." We can see this literally taking place in this story, as the children are in danger of becoming the indentured slaves of the lender. Talk about a stressful situation!

We don't know the late husband's name, but we do know a couple of other things about him. First, we know that he revered the Lord. In fact, he was "from the prophets of his day." This should remind us that even godly men can make financial mistakes.

Second, we know that he left no business or personal assets that could be sold to pay back the debt. This seems to indicate that he did not spend lavishly. Possibly he had borrowed to meet the needs of his family during one of the famines that occurred during this period, so we dare not stand in judgment of his motives. But whether or not his reasons for incurring debt were justified, the debt he left has put his widow and children in a precarious position.

A Culture of Debt

In generations past, failure to repay a loan could land the debtor in prison, so people feared debt. When credit cards were introduced, attitudes began to change. Gradually our society has shifted from acceptance of the use of debt to virtual dependence on debt. Today, consumers can purchase a home, a car, a college education, a vacation, or a pizza by using debt. Once dependence upon debt becomes a way of life, excessive borrowing is difficult to avoid. Debt is often the first option considered when making a purchase.

While writing this manuscript, I received a call from a 76-year-old widow desperately seeking my financial counsel. As she described the circumstances of her financial stress, my heart grew heavy. She had accumulated unsecured consumer debt of $180,000. Her retirement income from Social Security and pensions was $36,000 per year, but she had a mortgage payment that was nearly half of her income. By the time she paid her mortgage and living expenses, she had no money available to pay any of her creditors. Over the years, little debts had become massive debts. Now, due to her inability to repay her loans, she was facing bankruptcy, the loss of her home, and the loss of her fragile health.

Consequences

Debt is borrowing from our tomorrows to pay for our todays. When we decide to presume upon the future rather than wait upon God, we interfere with his ways of providing for our needs. While it is not a sin to borrow money, it is a sin to borrow and not repay. Psalm 37:21 says, *"The wicked borrow and do not repay."*

The high cost of debt can be measured in many ways:

• Interest Costs

Consumer credit interest rates are very expensive. It is far more economical to pay cash for a purchase.

• **Emotional Costs**

Excessive debt creates heavy stress. In some recent surveys, soldiers on active duty ranked financial stress greater than the stress they experience in combat.

• **Relational Costs**

Excessive debt destroys reputations, partnerships, business opportunities, marriages, and friendships.

• **Spiritual Costs**

Debt often inhibits our liberty to follow God's will. When we are encumbered by debt, we are not totally free to respond to God's leading. We can miss opportunities to serve God's purposes when we have two masters.

How to Avoid the Trap of Excessive Debt

God mercifully provided a way of escape for this helpless widow and her beloved children. We have much to learn from her experience, which is described in the following verses:

Elisha replied to her, "How can I help you? Tell me, what do you have in your house?"

"Your servant has nothing there at all," she said, "except a small jar of olive oil."

Elisha said, "Go around and ask all your neighbors for empty jars. Don't ask for just a few. Then go inside and shut the door behind you and your sons. Pour oil into all the jars, and as each is filled, put it to one side."

She left him and shut the door behind her and her sons. They

brought the jars to her and she kept pouring. When all the
jars were full, she said to her son, "Bring me another one."

But he replied, "There is not a jar left." Then the oil
stopped flowing.

She went and told the man of God, and he said, "Go, sell the
oil and pay your debts. You and your sons can live on
what is left."

(2 Kings 4:2-7)

Let's take a look at what happened:

First, the widow cried out to the man of God for help. This was a sign of her dependence upon God and his kindness. God answered her prayer by giving her a plan, communicated by the man of God, which would enable her to experience God's miraculous provision.

Second, notice that the widow had to do her part before God would do his part. Although the widow had said she had "nothing," in reality she had two important assets: a little oil and a community of people willing to help her. Before God provided more, the widow had to become a faithful steward of what she already had.

Third, the widow had to go to work to sell her oil. God did not simply fill her jars with money. He honors our efforts when we work.

Fourth, God provided in abundance so the widow could pay her debts, liberate her children, and survive her uncertain future. He often demonstrates his kindness most dramatically when we are most needy.

The first short film in the *God Provides*® series, "Widow and Oil" is a poignant retelling of this powerful story from 2 Kings 4. More information is available at www.crown.org.

APPLICATION

If you have excessive debt, make a plan to get totally debt free. Do not saddle your heirs with the stress of outstanding, unsecured financial obligations. At a minimum, take the following steps:

- Learn to patiently save money.
- Wait upon the Lord to provide.
- Pay cash for all purchases so as to avoid future debt.
- Implement the Debt Snowball strategy below to eliminate all consumer debt as soon as possible.

THE SNOWBALL STRATEGY

Choose the strategy option that best addresses your situation:

a) Pay off your smallest credit card debt, or
b) Pay off the card with the highest interest rate.

Then—

- Pay the minimum balances on your other cards, and focus on accelerating repayment of your smallest balance (option "a") or highest interest rate credit card (option "b").
- After you pay off the first credit card, apply its payment toward the next smallest (or next highest interesting rate) one.
- After you have paid off all your credit cards, focus on paying off your consumer debts in exactly the same way.

chapter

Materialism

Change What Impresses Us

ECCLESIASTES 2:1-11

olomon, the wisest and richest man to ever live, came up with an idea about how to use his vast wealth:

> *I thought in my heart, 'Come now, I will test you*
> *with pleasure to find out what is good.'*
>
> (Ecclesiastes 2:1)

Solomon wanted to know if money can buy happiness, so he invested time and money in an experiment in total self-indulgence. This idea seems to have simply popped into his head; we have no evidence he discussed it with others. But we do know from his own words that he conducted his investigation wholeheartedly: *"I denied myself nothing my eyes desired; I refused my heart no pleasure."* (v. 10)

In Ecclesiastes 2:2-10, Solomon tells us that he tested the following sources of happiness:

Laughter	➔ Amusement
Wine & Folly	➔ Drinking & Partying
Houses & Vineyards	➔ Growing and Tending Projects
Reservoirs to Water the Groves	➔ Building and Maintaining Projects
Male and Female Slaves	➔ Servants to Bring Ease and Comfort
Herds and Flocks	➔ Livestock Projects. Investments
Silver & Gold	➔ Financial Security. Investments
Men & Women Singers	➔ Entertainment
Harem	➔ Sexual Pleasures

His experiment ended in failure. The notion that money can buy happiness is an ancient myth that continues to fool people even today. Nevertheless, Solomon's efforts were not without merit, because we can learn much from his mistakes.

MODERN MATERIALISM

Solomon's self-indulgent search for personal happiness may seem quite bizarre to us, but don't be too quick to dismiss him as an odd duck. My work in financial stewardship puts me in contact with thousands of people every year, and I have found that rich and poor alike make Solomon's mistake. I've seen celebrities, business leaders, politicians, investors, pastors, a retired professional football player with two Super Bowl rings and even people whose home was an 8' x 8' hovel with dirt floors and a rusted tin roof fall victim to this subtle trap. The desire for more tempts us all.

As my friend Randy Alcorn says, "Satan is the Lord of Materialism." The enemy of our soul will use any and every strategy to deceive, misdirect, preoccupy, and divert believers. He wants us to become preoccupied with the things of this world, so we will lose our passion for the things of God.

NOTHING GAINED

We now know "the rest of the story" about Solomon's search for happiness. After spending lavishly on his own pleasures, he described the results of his experiment with these poignant words:

> *Yet, when I surveyed all that my hands had done and what I had toiled to achieve, everything was meaningless, a chasing after the wind; nothing was gained under the sun.*
> (Ecclesiastes 2:11)

We can become wiser than Solomon by learning from his mistakes. The idea that happiness can be found in material goods and pleasures is the ultimate deception. Chasing worldly happiness is a futile waste of time, money, talents, and energy. It drives men and women to orbit their lives around that which is temporal and fleeting. The cost is terribly high.

There is no lasting gain in building a private "thingdom." The Lord graciously reminds us many times in his word that such pursuits are meaningless. He warns us that one day every material thing will be destroyed:

> *But the day of the Lord will come like a thief. The heavens will disappear with a roar; the elements will be destroyed by fire, and the earth and everything done in it will be laid bare.*
>
> (2 Peter 3:10)

EMPTINESS

The life of Teddy Forstmann is a tragic example of excess materialism. A pioneer in the private-equity industry, his business acumen led him to become one of the richest men in the world. Those who revered his ability to turn companies around and reap massive financial windfalls considered him to be a "Master of the Universe." He was also a very active playboy in search of someone to love.

You can read the best account of his tragic life in Rich Cohen's *Vanity Fair* article titled "The Ghost in the Gulfstream." It chronicles the journey of a man who "could have had it all," but who ended up with nothing of real value. All that remained at the end of his lonely life was a trail of broken relationships. He was a friendless, lonely man jetting across the world in opulent luxury, yet living like a ghost.

There's no greater financial mistake than thinking money can buy happiness. That's a lie of the enemy. Material things have never brought lasting happiness, and they never will. Materialism brings misery, waste, and emptiness.

How to Avoid the Trap of Materialism

What impresses you? To avoid the pitfall of materialism, you need to answer this question with brutal honesty.

You are captivated by what most impresses you. The desires of your heart grow from the seeds you plant in your mind. The allures of the world constantly call out to you with tantalizing promises of comfort, pleasure, power, and prestige. They approach you as beautiful, well-packaged opportunities to satisfy your unmet needs.

Like me, many men are impressed with sports. As we grow older and transition from players to enthusiasts, this source of pleasure can turn into an obsession. Before we realize it, we're spending far too much time and money on activities that should occupy far less of a place in our lives. This can happen whether it is playing golf, hunting and fishing, skydiving, mountain climbing or watching sporting events on TV while playing fantasy football.

Women can be just as materialistic. Their obsessions might be shopping, beauty, movies, fashions, home furnishings, financial security, and other things that are not bad in themselves. But these attractions can easily become idols that cause the heart to wander away from God.

The enemy of our soul wants us to love the things of this world. God wants us to love him and him only. The Apostle John challenges us with these words:

> *Do not love the world or anything in the world. If anyone*
> *loves the world, love for the Father is not in them. For*
> *everything in the world—the lust of the flesh, the lust of the*
> *eyes, and the pride of life—comes not from the Father but*
> *from the world. The world and its desires pass away, but*
> *whoever does the will of God lives forever.*
>
> (1 John 2:15-17)

In this passage, John identifies the root causes of materialism:

- the desire to satisfy our flesh with pleasure
- the desire to have what attracts our eyes and stimulates our imagination
- the pride we develop as a result of what we have or do

Materialism is an indication that we are impressed by things more than God. It is idolatry. God considers it spiritual adultery.

> *Dear children, keep yourselves from idols.*
> (1 John 5:21)

> *You adulterous people, don't you know that friendship with the world is hatred toward God?*
> (James 4:4a)

chapter 7

APPLICATION

What most impresses you in other people? Success? Intelligence? Wealth? Attractiveness? Are you more impressed with Jesus than with the most impressive people you know? What qualities in Jesus do you most admire? Is your love and admiration for him constantly growing?

What material things impress you? Big houses? Fine cars? Luxurious vacations? Business profits? Are you more impressed with these earthly things than with heavenly things? What do you wake up thinking about in the morning?

If you have difficulty answering the above questions, perhaps you need to evaluate your priorities and make some adjustments. Test your need for spiritual realignment by looking over your calendar and your checkbook.

The antidote for materialism is being impressed with Christ and his kingdom. If he has not captivated your heart and mind, ask him to reveal more of himself to you. Make it your intention to turn away from the things of this world and focus more of your attention on him and his kingdom. Keep a journal of all the ways Christ impresses you in a day, a week or over the course of a year.

You will be shocked at how quickly the temporal things that impress you will dissipate. The things of this world will truly pale in comparison to him.

So we fix our eyes not on what is seen, but on what is unseen.
For what is seen is temporary, but what is unseen is eternal.

(2 Corinthians 4:18)

chapter

Funding Disobedience

Obey God's Call No Matter the Cost

Jonah 1

e all know that Jonah was swallowed by a great fish, which after keeping him for three days and nights inside its slimy belly, unceremoniously regurgitated him upon dry land. What an unforgettable experience the Lord devised to get his attention!

In this remarkable biblical account, we learn the reason for the prophet's round-trip journey to the bottom of the ocean. Jonah was running away from God's call on his life. It's important to note that the availability of money made it easier for him to disobey. Here's how his financial mistake is recorded in Jonah 1:1-2:

> *The word of the Lord came to Jonah son of Amittai: "Go to the great city of Nineveh and preach against it, because its wickedness has come up before me." But Jonah ran away from the Lord and headed for Tarshish. He went down to Joppa, where he found a ship bound for that port.* **After paying the fare**, *he went aboard and sailed for Tarshish to flee from the Lord.*

This reference to Jonah's financial decision has significant implications for us today. More often than we care to admit, Christians use their financial resources in a manner that promotes disobedience to God.

THE SIGN OF JONAH

While inside the great fish, Jonah repented of his attempt to run from God's assignment. His prayer acknowledges his desperate need for rescue and expresses his gratitude for God's mercy. It is clear that he understands the danger of the idolatry practiced by the sailors who prayed to their false gods for help that did not come.

> *Those who cling to worthless idols forfeit the grace that could be theirs, But I, with a song of thanksgiving, will sacrifice to you. What I have vowed I will make good. Salvation comes from the Lord.*
>
> (Jonah 2:8-9)

Jesus referred to this incident twice in the gospel of Matthew and once in the gospel of Luke as "the sign of Jonah":

> *Then some of the Pharisees and teachers of the law said to him, "Teacher, we want to see a sign from you."*
>
> *He answered, "A wicked and adulterous generation asks for a sign! But none will be given it except the sign of the prophet Jonah. For as Jonah was three days and three nights in the belly of a huge fish, so the Son of Man will be three days and three nights in the heart of the earth. The men of Nineveh will stand up at the judgment with this generation and condemn it; for they repented at the preaching of Jonah, and now something greater than Jonah is here."*
>
> (Matthew 12:38-41)

Jesus is telling these skeptics that he is a type of Jonah. He told them that he would descend into the earth for three days and nights, and after rising from the dead, he would call all people to turn from disobedience to obedience, from idolatry to faith in him.

Have you ever committed Jonah's mistake? That is, have you ever attempted to use your financial resources to fund your disobedience to God? I suspect most of us would unhesitatingly deny that we have been guilty of such obvious foolishness. But in the modern world, we can commit this error quite often without realizing it.

As you read the following parable Jesus told about a great banquet, note the excuses given by those who chose not to attend.

> *Jesus replied: "A certain man was preparing a great banquet and invited many guests. At the time of the banquet he sent his servant to tell those who had been invited, 'Come, for everything is now ready.'*
>
> *"But they all alike began to make excuses. The first said, 'I have just bought a field, and I must go and see it. Please excuse me.'*

*"Another said, 'I have just **bought five yoke of oxen**, and I'm*
on my way to try them out. Please excuse me.'

"Still another said, 'I just got married, so I can't come.'
"The servant came back and reported this to his master.
Then the owner of the house became angry and ordered his
servant, 'Go out quickly into the streets and alleys of the
town and bring in the poor, the crippled, the blind
and the lame.'

"'Sir,' the servant said, 'what you ordered has been done,
but there is still room.'

"Then the master told his servant, 'Go out to the roads and
country lanes and compel them to come in, so that my house
will be full. I tell you, not one of those who were invited
will get a taste of my banquet.'"

(Luke 14:16-24)

Each person had some excuse. The busyness of everyday life prevented them from responding to God's call. However, two-thirds of the excuses were made by people who let their money and possessions distract them. They allowed financial considerations to negatively influence their decision. Just as Jonah used his resources to purchase a ticket to sail to a distant land, they used their resources to build a case for not accepting the master's invitation.

CONSEQUENCES

Jonah's attempt to run from God resulted in a horrifying trip to the bottom of the ocean, a frightening imprisonment inside the belly of a whale, and a crash landing on a beach. God designed this extreme experience to lead him to repentance.

With this story of Jonah as a reference point, Jesus warns his listeners of the consequences that will come to those who allow money, possessions, and other distractions to keep them from heeding his call. He concluded the parable by saying, "...*not one of those invited* [but who refused to come] *will get a taste of my banquet.*"

All of our financial decisions have gravity. The time and attention they require can distract us from listening to and obeying God. When financial resources are available to us, we can be tempted to do things our way and in our own strength, rather than in dependence on God and in accordance with his will. The Bible makes it clear that handling money is a weighty responsibility:

> *The wages of the righteous bring them life, but the income of the wicked brings them punishment.*
>
> (Proverbs 10:16)

The availability of money opens doors to more opportunities, and it's easy to use these options as excuses. When we have access to adequate resources to do what we want, we may not wait on God to confirm his will and supply our needs.

HOW TO AVOID THE TRAP OF DISOBEDIENCE

To avoid the trap of disobedience, we must recognize our identity as citizens of heaven and operate from that perspective. Many business people struggle with decision making, because they are confused about their identity.

I often ask people the following simple question to help them clarify their identity: "Are you a Christian practicing business, or are you a businessman practicing Christianity?" Of course, the first answer is the correct one. But in the pressures of daily living, many Christians get confused. They don't know who they are, and they don't have clear priorities.

When we know who we are, we can make better decisions about what we should do in every area of our life, regardless of our vocation or mission. But we need to keep in mind that there is always a cost associated with obedience to the Lord's call.

When God clearly calls us to undertake an endeavor, we must be willing to count the cost then invest the resources required for obedience. We are told in 2 Samuel 24:24 how King David modeled this principle:

> *But the king replied to Araunah, "No, I insist on paying you for it.* ***I will not sacrifice to the Lord my God burnt offerings that cost me nothing."*** *So David bought the threshing floor and the oxen and paid fifty shekels of silver for them.*

Larry Burkett, Crown's late founder, became a Christian as an adult. He knew he was lacking in biblical knowledge and training, so he made a request and a promise to Jesus Christ that shaped his every decision. He said, "Lord, I am ignorant and a child in the faith. You will have to tolerate my ignorance as I grow and mature. But if you will make your will known to me, you will never have to put up with my disobedience."

We all need this same heart attitude. We need to be willing to surrender our own plans, agenda, and desires, so we can steadfastly walk in the path God has for us, regardless of where it may lead or what it may cost. When God called Larry to start a ministry teaching Christian financial principles, Larry freed up the necessary time by gracefully surrendering his ownership in a small business to his partner. It cost him money to walk away, but he knew he was being obedient by fully trusting God with his future.

To avoid the financial mistake of disobedience, we must be constantly vigilant and sensitive to the Holy Spirit. Paul spoke to this issue in Ephesians 5:15-17:

> *Be very careful, then, how you live—not as unwise but as wise, making the most of every opportunity, because the days are evil. Therefore do not be foolish, but understand what the Lord's will is.*

APPLICATION

Take an inventory of how you are using your resources of time, talent, and money. Divide them into two categories: Investments in God's Kingdom, Investments in My Kingdom. Don't feel guilty if the majority of your time is spent earning a living and raising your family. These are kingdom investments when approached with the motive to serve others and glorify God.

Ask God to reveal to you any areas where you have been disobedient to his call. Where have you been too busy or distracted by money and possessions to wholeheartedly respond to his leading?

Are you operating as a citizen of heaven or as a citizen of the world?

You are never too young or too old to begin living a life of obedience to the Lord, no matter how long or how far you may have wandered from him in the past.

chapter

Robbing God

*Make God's Financial Priorities
Our Priorities*

MALACHI 3

ou and I would likely be aghast if charged with the crime of robbing a bank or stealing someone else's property. But this is just the type of felony charge the prophet Malachi leveled against the Israelites. Adding to the seriousness, the stolen property was not man's, but God's!

Will a mere mortal rob God? Yet you rob me.

(Malachi 3:8)

Put yourself in the shoes of the Israelites. Can you imagine the weight of these words? The God of the universe addressing his subjects as "mere mortals" and charging them with robbery of his property! Thinking of it makes my knees weak, but the Israelites were unyielding, covering their sin by explaining that they were confused. They asked God how they were robbing him, and he answered them: *"In tithes and offerings."* (v. 9)

God had commanded the Israelites to give both tithes and offerings to support the work of the priests, so they would have the resources to teach his truth to the people. Without knowledge of God's commands and principles, the Israelites would be unable to fulfill their purpose as his chosen people. In calling the Israelites robbers, he was not merely condemning a bad attitude. He was stating that their bad behavior had tangible, quantifiable effects. When confronted so clearly and directly, the guilty had no place to hide.

TO TITHE OR NOT TO TITHE

When God fulfilled the law through the life, death, and resurrection of Jesus Christ, he established a new covenant of grace and ushered in a new standard of giving. As Christians, we are free to give according to our ability as led by the Holy Spirit.

When God fulfilled the law, he raised the standards; he did not lower them. So we must be careful not to use our freedom as an excuse to rob God. As Randy Alcorn points out, "If we were required to tithe under the law, how much more should we joyfully give under the covenant of grace!" But the data suggests that we continue to operate more like these Israelites.

During the last half-century in America, increased wealth has coincided with decreased giving. Pollster George Barna writes, "Generally, the more money a person makes the less likely he is to tithe." Indeed, giving levels were higher during the Great Depression of the 1930s, when incomes were low compared to today. [i]

CONSEQUENCES

The people didn't have to speculate about the consequences of robbing God. Malachi 3:9 states bluntly: *"You are under a curse—your whole nation—because you are robbing me."*

While the verses that follow do not explicitly specify the nature of the curse, they seem to indicate that God will cease to bless their crops and fields. In other words, withholding money from God brings negative financial and economic consequences upon the people.

HOW TO AVOID THE TRAP OF ROBBING GOD

God is gracious as well as just. He did not leave the Israelites in despair over their guilt, nor did he immediately execute judgment by withholding his blessings. Rather, he graciously gave them specific instructions for correcting their sinful behavior:

> *"Bring the whole tithe into the storehouse, that there may be food in my house."*

God directed the people to once again give a tenth of their crops/income to the priests who managed the temple, his house. Note that the solution begins with simple obedience in the area of giving.

> *"Test me in this," says the Lord Almighty...*

God invites the Israelites to put him to a test! This no doubt sounded outrageous to the people, because Deuteronomy 6:16 says, *"Do not test the*

Lord your God as you did at Massah." Jesus quoted this verse to Satan when Satan tempted him to jump from the highest point of the temple to prove that God was trustworthy. But in this case, God was addressing the core issue that had stagnated the generosity of his people…they did not trust him.

I've heard people say, "If God would give me a large sum of money, I'd be happy to be generous with it." In essence, they're inviting God to test their trustworthiness. But God does not respond to this wishful thinking and upside-down logic. He turns the tables and says that we must first trust him by being generous. The test is not of his faithfulness but of our confidence in him.

After the testing, God makes an incredible offer to experience his generosity:

> *"and see if I will not throw open the floodgates of heaven and pour out so much blessing that there will not be room enough to store it. I will prevent pests from devouring your crops, and the vines in your fields will not drop their fruit before it is ripe," says the Lord Almighty. "Then all the nations will call you blessed, for yours will be a delightful land," says the Lord Almighty.* (v. 10-12)

This passage is not the prosperity gospel, the heresy that we should demand of God to make us rich, or give to God in order to get something back. This is the divine law of generosity, which says that we must give by faith while trusting completely in God to provide for our own needs.

Faith in action is putting our money where our mouth is. If we say we trust God, then we need to actually trust him by being generous towards him and others with a pure heart, knowing that God is not blind to our personal needs.

APPLICATION

Begin giving God 10 percent of your gross annual income each year. Do this without expectation to gain material benefit in return. Trust God to provide for your needs according to his promises. Keep a journal of God's faithfulness. Go ahead. Test him!

---

[i] http://library.generousgiving.org/page.asp?sec=4&page=161

Compromising Our Mission

*Recognize and Reject
Satan's Generosity*

Matthew 4:1-11

ive is an incredibly powerful verb! Our ears perk up when someone makes an offer to give us something of value. Not long ago, that verb jumped off the pages of my Bible in the context of the temptations of Christ. How amazing that Satan actually made an offer to "give" the Lord of the Universe all "the kingdoms of the world"!

Again, the devil took him to a very high mountain and
showed him all the kingdoms of the world and their splendor.
"All this I will give you," he said, "if you will bow down and
worship me."
(Matthew 4:8-9)

Satan's generous offer had a not-so-subtle string attached to it. Jesus would have to compromise his mission, which was ultimately to redeem the world from Satan's control. No wonder Beelzebub, as he is known elsewhere[1], made the highest and best offer he could possibly muster. Today we may marvel when business deals involve billions of dollars, but the stakes in this negotiation involved control of the entire world. To win this prize, Jesus only had to bow down and worship the Great Deceiver. But he didn't!

Jesus said to him, "Away from me, Satan! For it is written:
'Worship the Lord your God, and serve him only.'" (v. 10)

In saying no to Satan, Jesus avoided making the worst financial mistake of all time. We are the beneficiaries of his wise and courageous response to Satan, but the enemy of our souls is not out of business. He continually offers to give each of us more of the world, if we will only compromise our mission. Tragically, these deceptive offers are easier to recognize when they are presented to others. It is much more difficult to recognize temptation when we're on the receiving end.

MISSION COMPROMISE

Satan often wins this battle to negotiate a compromise. Consider the outrageous actions of Ari Mandel, a formerly Orthodox Jew who decided that his good deeds had earned him a place in heaven. He did not want it, however. He preferred to have cash in hand to enjoy the pleasures available in this life, so he put his personal spot in heaven up for auction on eBay. The bids reached $100,000 before eBay shut down the auction for violating their policy against selling intangible things. While this looks ridiculous at face value, in practice many today live in the same way. We forfeit our eternal rewards in pursuit of the generous temporal riches that we desire now.

On the other hand, there are cases where Satan obviously loses the negotiation. Millard Fuller is the late founder of Habitat for Humanity, the not-for-profit organization that provides housing for low-income Americans. He had a successful career in business prior to launching his charity, but this success nearly cost him everything. In spite of being a young millionaire, his health, integrity, and marriage were suffering. He recognized that he had been captive to Satan's generosity. To overcome this threat, he and his wife sold everything they had and committed themselves to radically follow Jesus.

Satan's mission is to keep Christians from fulfilling their God-given missions. One of his chief methods is to tempt us with the stronghold of luxury. He is delighted when we go about doing good, acquiring wealth, and increasing comfort and pleasures, because while that is happening, often our real purpose goes unfulfilled. The Apostle James strives to shake us out of our complacency with these strong words:

> *For the sun rises with scorching heat and withers the plant;*
> *its blossom falls and its beauty is destroyed. In the same way,*
> *the rich will fade away even while they go*
> *about their business.*
> (James 1:11)

CONSEQUENCES

If we accept Satan's business deal to exchange eternal joy for temporal pleasures, we compromise our true mission. We gain nothing except the possibility of applause from men, the fleeting sense of control or power, and the satisfaction of indulging our passions for a season.

The real consequences of falling into this temptation are difficult to quantify, but we can get some idea from these passages:

*For the love of money is a root of all kinds of evil. Some people, **eager for money**, have wandered from the faith and pierced themselves with many griefs.*

(1 Timothy 6:10)

*But mark this: There will be terrible times in the last days. People will be lovers of themselves, **lovers of money**, boastful, proud, abusive, disobedient to their parents, ungrateful, unholy, without love, unforgiving, slanderous, without self-control, brutal, not lovers of the good, treacherous, rash, conceited, lovers of pleasure rather than lovers of God— having a form of godliness but denying its power. Have nothing to do with such people.*

(2 Timothy 3:1-5)

HOW TO AVOID THE TRAP OF COMPROMISE

Our Lord withstood the devil's temptations in three ways:

First, Jesus was clear about his mission. He knew that Satan's offer of gaining the world conflicted with his mission of freeing the world, which he publically announced by reading from the scroll of Isaiah in the synagogue:

He went to Nazareth, where he had been brought up, and on the Sabbath day he went into the synagogue, as was his custom. He stood up to read, and the scroll of the prophet Isaiah was handed to him. Unrolling it, he found the place where it is written:

"The Spirit of the Lord is on me,
because he has anointed me
to proclaim good news to the poor.
He has sent me to proclaim freedom for the prisoners
and recovery of sight for the blind,
to set the oppressed free,
to proclaim the year of the Lord's favor."
(Luke 4:16-19)

Second, Jesus recognized Satan's offer as a lie. Because he knew God's Word, he knew that Satan was tempting him to deviate from it.

Third, Jesus quoted God's Word to Satan. In so doing, he expressed his allegiance to God's plans for his life. He was fully confident in God's faithfulness to his promises, and he relied upon them during times of testing.

We must prepare ourselves to use the same three-step defense system. Our mission on earth is to carry out the mission that Jesus began. Whether we are a businessperson, a fulltime wife and mother, a student, a scientist, an artist, a manual laborer, a doctor, a soldier, or in some other station in life, the true purpose of our life is the same: to work for the coming of God's Kingdom in the way that he purposed for us.

chapter

APPLICATION

Write a personal mission statement that is supported by scripture. After you have clarified your calling, list ways you can better focus on fulfilling it at the place where you are presently working or serving.

Honestly assess whether you are compromising your true mission in any way.

Determine if you have been a victim of Satan's generosity.

If you do not know your God given identity or your destiny to fulfill the good works God created in advance for you to accomplish, I highly recommend that you contact Crown to speak with a Career Direct Consultant. We can help you understand your God-given design and point you to the field of study or career that will align with your unique design.

---

[1] Matthew 10:25, 12:24, 12:27 and other places

Storing Up Treasures on Earth

Store Up Treasures in Heaven

LUKE 12:16-21

he Bible contains a poignant story that I call the "Parable of the American Dream." Jesus begins it as follows:

> *The ground of a certain rich man yielded an abundant harvest. He thought to himself, "What shall I do? I have no place to store my crops." Then he said, "This is what I'll do. I will tear down my barns and build bigger ones, and there I will store my surplus grain. And I'll say to myself, 'You have plenty of grain laid up for many years. Take life easy; eat, drink and be merry.'"*
>
> (Luke 12:16-19)

This man has managed his business so well that he had no place to store all of his production. Being a forward-thinking businessman, he solves the problem by taking the following actions:

- He develops a plan to raze the existing facility and build on the same real estate a new facility with sufficient storage to provide for a comfortable retirement.

- Without consulting anyone, he develops a retirement plan that will allow him to "eat, drink, and be merry." Although he doesn't mention playing golf or "sailing to nowhere" on his yacht, he no doubt has similar diversions in mind.

Do you know anyone who acts like this foolish rich man? Actually, millions of people do. They come from all income levels and nationalities. Their story might more accurately be called the "Parable of the Retirement Dream."

MODERN RETIREMENT PLANS

The retirement dream pretty much assumes that we will work hard for about two-thirds of our life to accumulate a surplus of assets, so we can spend the final one-third of our life doing whatever we want. Most people who pursue the retirement dream are longing for an end-of-life extended vacation. The entire financial planning industry is built around the notion that everyone has a right to a self-directed retirement.

I once read the account of a middle-aged couple whose business acumen enabled them to achieve the coveted status of financial independence earlier than most. Since they were young, healthy, and childless, they decided to buy a yacht and sail around the Caribbean, stopping occasionally to collect seashells and indulge their passion of playing in co-ed softball leagues on the beautiful islands.

Because our culture is so accustomed to thinking of retirement as an earned right, we may not see anything wrong with this couple's shallow, self-centered lifestyle. So, I'll mention another example to drive home the point. A few days after a horrific tsunami leveled Phuket Island, Thailand, killing thousands of people, BBC news dispatched a journalist to cover the story. His report gave me nausea.

When the journalist arrived at this once tranquil, luxurious vacation destination, bodies were still floating in the horrible muddy mess; survivors were grieving the loss of their loved ones, their homes, and their possessions. But strangely, the other side of the island only a few miles away was unaffected by the disaster, and the tourist industry was continuing as usual. He interviewed one British young man, sitting on the beach in swimsuit and sunglasses with a drink in his hand, who said something like, "Too bad for those who got caught in the tsunami, but fortunately for me, there is no damage here. The water is still blue, drinks are being served, and my vacation is not ruined in any way whatsoever. Cheers!"

If you had friends or children or relatives who were unaccounted for on Phuket Island, think about how concerned you would be about their safety, their access to medical attention, and even their access to clean water. How would you feel if you turned on the TV, hoping to learn about the rescue efforts, only to see this interview with the calloused, self-absorbed tourist?

While very few of us would act in a similar manner with regard to the needs of the world, we can fall into trap of thinking like the farmer who wanted bigger barns to indulge in a life of leisure.

CONSEQUENCES

Most financial planners consider failure to plan for retirement to be one of the biggest financial mistakes a person can make. An infinitely bigger mistake is to plan our lives selfishly, without regard for God's plan for our lives. No wonder Jesus concludes this parable with these strong words:

> *But God said to him, "You fool! This very night your life will*
> *be demanded from you. Then who will get what you have*
> *prepared for yourself?" This is how it will be with whoever*
> *stores up things for themselves but is not rich toward God.*
> (Luke 12:20-21)

The foolish businessman in Jesus' parable is much like the British tourist. Both are captivated by their desire for worldly pleasures, and both are oblivious to the pain and suffering that surrounds them. Jesus is not amused. He informs the foolish businessman that his retirement plans have been changed. Instead of years, he will have one day!

This parable warns us not to presume upon tomorrow. Each of us has only today. We are placed here on the earth for a purpose, and we should constantly be looking for how we can fulfill that purpose. We have a choice: We can either focus on ourselves and worldly possessions, in which case we will lose our soul, or we can "run the race that is marked out for us" and gain an eternal reward.

HOW TO AVOID THE TRAP OF STORING UP EARTHLY TREASURES

The Bible never condemns wealth, financial planning, or retirement. In fact, it instructs us to be careful planners, to create surplus for our families, and to provide an inheritance for our children and grandchildren. However, scripture does condemn wrong attitudes, selfish motives, and the misuse of the resources that God has entrusted to each of us.

"Rich fools," to use a Biblical term, will typically employ a variety of reasons to justify their behavior. I talked with one man who believed it was his responsibility to give each of his children a minimum inheritance of $10 million, so they would "have a head start in life." Another told me that upon his death he was leaving about 4 percent of his vast fortune to several charities. He thought this was being very generous, but actually he was investing 96% of his wealth in the American retirement dream. By giving some of his wealth to charity, I suppose he hoped to hedge his bets.

In Matthew 6:19-21, Jesus speaks with absolute clarity about what we should and should not do in order to avoid this financial mistake.

Do not store up for yourselves treasures on earth, where moths and vermin destroy, and where thieves break in and steal.

But store up for yourselves treasures in heaven, where moths and vermin do not destroy, and where thieves do not break in and steal. For where your treasure is, there your heart will be also.

How do we know if we are storing up treasures on earth? Here is a simple rule: If it can be stolen, eaten by moths, or destroyed by vermin, it falls into the category of worldly assets. That seems pretty clear, doesn't it?

But how do we go about laying up treasures in heaven? I'll suggest three ways:

1. We invest our time, talents, and resources in the advancement of the Great Commission as given by Jesus in Matthew 28:18-20:

   All authority in heaven and on earth has been given to me. Therefore go and make disciples of all nations, baptizing them in the name of the Father and of the Son and of the Holy Spirit, and teaching them to obey everything I have commanded you. And surely I am with you always, to the very end of the age.

2. We serve the needs of the widow, the orphan, the sick, the poor, the alien, and the prisoner, as directed in Matthew 25 and other places.

3. We participate in the sufferings of Christ, so that we may be overjoyed when his glory is revealed. (1 Peter 4:13)

The actual nature of the "treasures" we are storing in heaven remains a mystery. Moses was looking for them; the saints in Hebrews 10 were looking for them; and Paul was looking for them. We don't know exactly what they're like, but this much we know: God promises that our eternal riches will surpass all the treasures we could ever accumulate on earth, no matter how many barns are required to store them.

chapter

APPLICATION

- Surrender all of your life to God's ownership and control.

- Consider yourself an alien and stranger on earth.

- Commit to make laying up treasures in heaven your greatest financial priority.

- Find the right balance between the lifestyle you chose, the inheritance you establish for your children and grandchildren, and the investments you make in God's kingdom.

- Plan on repurposing (not retiring) the use of your time and money in your senior years to maximize your impact on others.

Self-Indulgence

*Open Our Eyes to the Needs
That Surround Us*

LUKE 16:19-31

he road to hell is commonly thought to be paved with self-destructive behaviors brought on by drugs, alcohol, promiscuity, or criminal activities. It is far less common to think of it being paved with luxury.

The devoutly religious Pharisees are described in Luke 16 as having three deeply rooted problems with regard to self-indulgence:

1. They loved money.

2. They overtly rejected the teachings of Christ about money, even going so far as to sneer at him.

3. They sought to justify their attitudes about money in the eyes of men, so they would not have to change their behaviors.

Jesus addressed their stubborn pride by telling a dramatic, intentionally disturbing story of an unnamed "rich man" in Luke 16:

> *There was a rich man who dressed in purple and fine linen*
> *and lived in luxury every day.* (v. 19)

So far, the story contains nothing to offend. Note that Jesus does not condemn this man for his wealth. As the story continues, however, we learn about the impact his lifestyle choices have on others:

> *At his gate was laid a beggar named Lazarus, covered with*
> *sores and longing to eat what fell from the rich man's table.*
> *Even the dogs came and licked his sores.* (v. 20-21)

Now the problem becomes clear. In full view of the rich man was a poor man who was sick and starving. Lazarus is outside the physical gate. Of far more significance, he is outside the emotional and spiritual concerns of the rich man. The story quickly ratchets up to an incredible climax, which reveals the eternal consequences this hardhearted tycoon suffered for his ugly callousness and loathing selfishness:

> *The time came when the beggar died and the angels carried*
> *him to Abraham's side. The rich man also died and was buried.*
> *In hell, where he was burning in torment, he looked up and*
> *saw Abraham far away, with Lazarus by his side.* (v. 22-23)

Pause for a second and consider the scene. The self-justifying Pharisees, the very descendants of Abraham, are listening to an account of a poor man ushered by angels into the presence of the patriarch of their faith, while the rich man is in the torment of hell. Jesus has turned the tables on his listeners. These Pharisees must have been waiting in stunned silence to see how the story unfolds.

The rich man, who was accustomed to being served while on earth, pleads for Lazarus to serve him, even while he is in hell! Abraham rejects that request with these piercing words:

> *Son, remember that in your lifetime you received your good things, while Lazarus received bad things, but now he is in comforted here and you are in agony.* (v. 25)

Moral of the story: Things matter; choices matter; lifestyles matter.

LIFESTYLE CHOICES

The Bible describes many bad types of financial decisions that we are prone to make. But convincing ourselves that we need, deserve, and "must have" an abundance of personal comforts is perhaps the most common and most easily rationalized. A friend of mine once observed that the "desire for pleasure and comfort is the most challenging of all addictions to break."

To gauge the truth of his statement, we need only look at the continual financial upgrades that characterize most of our lives. We start with a small house, a functional car, and simple furnishings that we can manage on a modest income. Over time, we move into a bigger house with excess furnishings and multiple cars, which require ever-higher incomes to maintain. Once started, this cycle keeps going, and we find ourselves on a perpetual quest for more:

> *Whoever loves money never has enough; whoever loves wealth is never satisfied with their income. This too is meaningless.*
> (Ecclesiastes 5:10)

The "mini-storage unit" industry generates an average of $24 billion per year, which is reportedly more than the value of the items stored in the units. It also has been one of the fastest growing industries in America for the past four decades.

It is not just Americans who suffer with the desire to accumulate, while remaining indifferent to the needs that surround us. The following description of this dichotomy is taken from an article titled "Billionaires and Beggars," in a 2008 issue of *The Guardian*:

> "In quieter times, the entrance lobby to the Taj Palace hotel acts as a gateway between two Indias. As they approach the building on foot, visitors are hustled by women beggars proffering their skeletal, scab-ridden babies for inspection. Tourists learn quickly to step over the corpse-like bodies, shrouded in blankets, who lie sleeping on the pavements. On the seafront just in front of the hotel, dust from endless construction sites and gritty pollution from the heaving traffic chokes the throat."

> "Enter the glass doors and there is jasmine-scented calm. Here, India's new business elite meet with their western contacts in pristine marble opulence. The hotel's management does everything to maintain the illusion that this is Mumbai, city of the future, the business capital of an emerging superpower. Inside there is no trace of the country's underclass. Representatives of the other Mumbai, the city of the destitute, the deprived, the downtrodden, are not allowed to cross the frontier." [1]

CONSEQUENCES

In Jesus' vivid story, Lazarus being placed outside the rich man's gate indicates that choosing all of the "good things" on earth for ourselves will lead to eternal agony. Of all the piercing words he uses, I especially hope I never hear these:

Remember, that in your lifetime, you received your good things....

A life lived for comfort and pleasure is a wasted life, temporally as well as eternally. Theodore Roosevelt, the 26th president of the United States, once said, "There has never been a man in history who pursued a life of leisure whose name is worth remembering." Can you prove him wrong by naming an exception?

We will never accomplish God's mission for our lives when our mission is comfort and pleasure. A self-indulgent lifestyle consumes our time, our creativity, and our energy. It distracts us from God's best. The Apostle Paul described the problem this way in 1 Timothy 6:9:

> *People who want to get rich fall into temptation and a trap*
> *and into many foolish and harmful desires that plunge men*
> *into ruin and destruction.*

HOW TO AVOID THE TRAP OF SELF-INDULGENCE

Most of us tend to compare what we have with what others have. We privately reason that if others in our income bracket have three cars with leather seats, it must not be self-indulgence for me to have three cars with cloth seats. If we've worked hard enough to get the money to pay for our lifestyle, it must be okay. The challenge is knowing where to draw the line.

In determining how much is enough, Jesus made a strong case for modest living when he compared the lifestyle choices of the rich man with the suffering of Lazarus. In 1 Timothy 6:7-8, Paul says the baseline is food and clothing; the rest is optional:

> *For we brought nothing into this world, and we take*
> *nothing out of it. But if we have food and clothing, we will*
> *be content with that.*

In Philippians 2:3-4, Paul comments further on what our priorities should be:

> *Do nothing out of selfish ambition or vain conceit. Rather,*
> *in humility value others above yourselves, not looking to your*
> *own interests but each of you to the interests of others.*

Too often, people must suffer a shock before they will open their eyes to the downside of self-indulgence. Don't wait for that shock to come. The real joy in life is recognizing and serving each Lazarus that God places outside of our own gate.

---

[1] Matthew 10:25, 12:24, 12:27 and other places

chapter

APPLICATION

- Find someone or some group near your home, in your church, or in your family that needs your compassionate support. Does a Lazarus in your life immediately come to your mind?

- Begin denying your personal desires and comforts to invest your time, talents, and treasures to improve the lives of others.

- Be on the lookout for those who are outside your own gates.

- Learn more about relational generosity and the incredible work of poverty elimination by The Open Table at www.theopentable.org.

For an impactful visual experience of Jesus' parable from Luke 16, view the short film "Rich Man and Lazarus," part of Crown's *God Provides*® series. More information is available at www.crown.org

Fearful Stewardship

Faithfully Use Every Talent for His Purposes

MATTHEW 25:14-30

 n the parables that he told to illustrate spiritual truths, Jesus frequently points out the positive consequences of obedience and the negative consequences of disobedience. In the parable of the talents, for example, the master offers praise and rewards for the actions of the two good servants, but harsh words and judgment for the one poor servant. Jesus starts the parable as follows:

> *Again, it will be like a man going on a journey, who called his servants and entrusted his wealth to them. To one he gave five talents of money to another two talents, and to another one talent, each according to his ability. Then he went on his journey.*

In today's vernacular, we might say this parable has to do with the "social economic strata" of the workplace. One servant is rich, one servant is "middle class," and one is poor. Jesus continues:

> *The man who had received five talents of money went at once and put his money to work and gained five talents more. So also, the one with two talents of money gained two more. But the man who had received one talent went off, dug a hole in the ground and hid his master's money.*

After a long time the master of these servants returned and settled accounts with them. The servant with five talents and the servant with two talents had each doubled their money. The master commended each of them with the following words:

> *"Well done, good and faithful servant! You have been faithful with a few things; I will put you in charge of many things. Come and share your master's happiness!"*

The servant entrusted with the single talent had a different story:

> *"Master," he said, "I knew that you are a hard man, harvesting where you have not sown and gathering where you have not scattered seed. So I was afraid and went out*

> *and hid your talent in the ground. See, here is what belongs*
> *to you."*

The master was not pleased:

> *His master replied, "You wicked, lazy servant! So you knew*
> *that I harvest where I have not sown and gather where I*
> *have not scattered seed? Well then, you should have put my*
> *money on deposit with the bankers, so that when I returned I*
> *would have received it back with interest. So take the talent*
> *of gold from him and give it to the one who has ten talents.*
> *For whoever has will be given more, and they will have an*
> *abundance. Whoever does not have, even what they have*
> *will be taken from them. And throw that worthless servant*
> *outside, into the darkness, where there will be weeping and*
> *gnashing of teeth."*

What a stern rebuke! This is the only place where Jesus speaks words of rebuke to the poor, so we should pay close attention to learn what this servant did wrong.

I believe he made at least two errors. First, he had a wrong belief about the owner of the talents:

> *"I knew that you are a hard man, harvesting where you*
> *have not sown and gathering where you have not scattered*
> *seed."*

Is this master really that mean? He is firm, but there is every indication that he is also fair and just. This servant clearly does not know, respect, and trust his master. This causes him to make bad decisions.

> *"So I was afraid and went out and hid your talent in the*
> *ground. See, here is what belongs to you."*

This servant's second mistake was unfaithfulness. He did not accomplish the mission his master had entrusted to him. We should not underestimate the devastating consequences of this decision. By burying the talent, the steward destroyed any opportunity for the asset to be used for good. He not only failed to use the talent for his master's purposes, he robbed others of the opportunity as well.

A Modern Parable

A Christian friend of mine gave a copy of the New Testament to his Jewish mother, and she agreed to read it out of respect for her son. But when she came to the parable of the talents, she so strongly disagreed with the way the master condemned the servant with the one talent that she could read no further. She just could not understand what this servant had done wrong.

My friend came to me for advice. After learning that his mother employed a financial manager to handle her investments, I suggested that he present to his mother the following scenario, which is really a modern version of Jesus' parable:

"Imagine that you choose three investment managers in order to diversify your portfolio. You give one manager $5 million, one $2 million, and another $1 million. After seven years, you ask them to report on their results.

"The first reports that the investment of $5 million that he managed is now worth $10 million, and the second reports that he has increased the assets under his care from $2 million to $4 million. However, the investment manager whom you entrusted with $1 million reports that he was afraid of losing the money and making you angry, so he kept the money hidden under his mattress. How would you feel about this third investment manager?"

About a week after he told this modern version of the parable to his mother, he called me and said, "Thanks so much for making the concept real to her. She gets it now! She wholeheartedly agrees that the third investment manager should have placed the money in a money market account, where it would have at least gained some small return from simple interest."

CONSEQUENCES

The fearful servant was guilty of mismanagement. That was a serious mistake, but it wasn't his most serious. His greatest mistake was unfaithfulness. He failed to accomplish the mission his master had assigned to him.

More money obviously is not this master's major need. He's already wealthy. He can do without the one talent and the potential to gain one more. The most important thing to this master is not money, but loyalty. He needs servants he can trust to carry out his instructions. When he distributed the money to the servants, he was essentially conducting a test to see who would be faithful. In a very real sense, every assignment in life is such a test.

Unfortunately, the servant who received one talent failed the test. The master called him a "wicked, lazy servant." Ouch! Then he took that one talent away from him and gave it to the servant with ten talents. Ouch! Ouch! This fearful servant lost his job, his reputation, and his relationship with his master. His wrong beliefs led him into utter ruin.

It should be painfully obvious that God is serious about our responsibility to be faithful investment managers of all that he has entrusted to us.

HOW TO AVOID THE TRAP OF FEARFUL STEWARDSHIP

On a number of occasions my wife has begun a conversation by saying, "You should have…..(fill in the blank)." When I hear those words, I brace myself for a painful, but usually necessary, correction.

I can't imagine ever hearing the words "you should have" from Jesus, but Jesus spoke those words to the fearful servant:

> *So you knew that I harvest where I have not sown and gather where I have not scattered seed? Well then, you should have put my money on deposit with the bankers, so that when I returned I would have received it back with interest.*

God is both kind and stern. He gives a generous measure of time, talents, and treasures to "each according to his ability." He expects us to use these gifts to accomplish his purposes. We must choose whether we will accept this responsibility. If we are unwilling to manage these assets for the benefit of his kingdom, we should transfer them to someone else who will. We should never bury them in the ground or hide them under our mattress.

We need to be faithful to God and intentional about our God-given purpose, regardless of whether we have much or little. As indicated in this parable, God expects us to take risks to gain a higher return for his kingdom. The Apostle Paul, who used his gifts to maximum effect and helped empower others to do the same, modeled this type of intentional living. In 1 Corinthians 9:24-27, he urges all of us to live our lives as if we are running a race:

> *Do you not know that in a race all the runners run, but only one gets the prize? Run in such a way as to get the prize. Everyone who competes in the games goes into strict training. They do it to get a crown that will not last, but we do it to get a crown that will last forever. Therefore I do not run like someone running aimlessly; I do not fight like a boxer beating the air. No, I strike a blow to my body and make it my slave so that after I have preached to others, I myself will not be disqualified for the prize.*

APPLICATION

In the area of financial stewardship, are you being faithful or fearful?

Start each year by asking yourself, "Is my life currently my very best response to the Great Commission? If I knew that I had only one year, one month or one week to live, what would I do differently?"

After some self-examination, make a plan to faithfully invest your time, talents, and treasure in ways and areas that will please the Lord. Take more risks knowing that God is pleased by our best efforts for his purposes. Do any new and exciting risks come to mind at this time?

Protecting Job Security

Recognize God as Our Provider

MATTHEW 26:14-16

he Pharisees were religious professionals. Their jobs gave them money, benefits, influence, and prestige. But when Jesus appeared on the scene, ushering in the kingdom of God, they realized their religious empire was threatened. They sought at every turn to discredit this religious upstart. But all of their attempts miserably failed.

Finally, desperate to maintain their job security, they devised a plan to end Jesus' life. In order to set this plot in motion, they would need an insider to serve as an escort for the Roman soldiers who would make the arrest. Satan, as if on cue, sent them just the man.

> *Then one of the Twelve —the one called Judas Iscariot — went to the chief priests and asked, "What are you willing to give me if I hand him over to you?"* (v. 14)

What motivated Judas to consider such a corrupt deed? The Bible specifically mentions at least one motivation: money. Perhaps after some negotiations, the chief priests and Judas settled on the amount of thirty silver coins for the betrayal. Once Judas had the money in hand, he set his heart on pleasing his new employer.

> *From then on Judas watched for an opportunity to hand him over.* (v. 16)

On the night of the betrayal, imagine the turmoil in Judas's mind as he is seated at the table sharing the Passover meal with the other disciples. Then, abruptly, Jesus ratchets up the intensity another notch:

> *And while they were eating, he said, "I tell you the truth, one of you will betray me."*

> *They were very sad and began to say to him one after the other, "Surely not I, Lord?"*

Judas's heart must have been pounding! His secret is no longer a secret. Jesus is aware of the coming betrayal! How did he find out? Does he know who will betray him?

> *Jesus replied, "The one who has dipped his hand into the bowl with me will betray me. The Son of Man will go just as it is written about him. But woe to that man who betrays the Son of Man! For it would be better for him if he had not been born."* (v. 20-23)

Judas's mind was racing. Should he rush back to the Pharisees and return the money? Should he confess and repent on the spot? What would you do? With thirty silver coins in his pocket, Judas boldly lied to Jesus' face.

> *Then Judas, the one who would betray him said, "Surely not I, Rabbi?" Jesus answered, "Yes, it is you."* (v. 25)

Oh, my! I would have been shaking in my boots at that moment. I hope that the conviction of my concealed sin now revealed would have bubbled over in an immediate reversal of my plans. But that's not what happened.

Judas had switched allegiances. It had taken only a token amount of money to seal his fate. His loyalty was now with the people who were paying him, not with the one he had once professed to follow. When Jesus gave him a chance to confess, Judas opted for job security.

Surely Not I

Job security is a powerful motivator. Richard Nixon was the most powerful man in the world when he was president of the United States. To protect his job, he compromised the law and hired spies to collect political information for his re-election advantage. When some began to discover his misdeeds, he lied to cover them up in what became known as the Watergate scandal.

There is a Judas lurking in every heart. Just as Judas's allegiance to his job with the Pharisees led to his downfall, President Nixon's efforts to protect his job security brought disgrace to him and our nation. We are all susceptible to this temptation. Let us guard against the arrogance and pride of thinking we have nothing to learn from Judas's terrible financial mistake.

I once counseled a young married couple that was drowning in debt only six months after their extravagant wedding. When I began to ask a series of questions about their income and expenses, I learned that both of them were working as full-time commissioned salespeople.

Inquiring deeper, I discovered that the husband had not made a single sale of his company's products since he began the job, but that he had turned in falsified reports to receive monthly income. His wife had tried without success to get him to confess this and pay restitution. Fearful of losing his job, he continued the deceitful thefts month after month.

The session became even more disturbing when I learned that he had also lied to his wife about his debt and income prior to their marriage. He was betraying his wife as well as his employer. I asked him to repent before God, and then to trust God as he sought to tell the truth and make right all his lies and misdeeds. He was not interested, and our counseling session abruptly ended. I later learned that the marriage ended as well.

"Surely not I" is a dangerous position to take on our personal vulnerability to the financial mistakes of Judas. Failure to acknowledge our sinful hearts can lead to our downfall.

CONSEQUENCES

Following his betrayal, Judas recognized the horror of his misdeed, which resulted in Jesus' death sentence. Pick up the account of the consequences of his sin in Matthew 27: 1- 10:

Early in the morning, all the chief priests and the elders of the people made their plans how to have Jesus executed. So they bound him, led him away and handed him over to Pilate the governor.

When Judas, who had betrayed him, saw that Jesus was condemned, he was seized with remorse and returned the thirty pieces of silver to the chief priests and the elders.

"I have sinned," he said, "for I have betrayed innocent blood."

"What is that to us?" they replied. "That's your responsibility." So Judas threw the money into the temple and left. Then he went away and hanged himself.

The chief priests picked up the coins and said, "It is against the law to put this into the treasury, since it is blood money." So they decided to use the money to buy the potter's field as a burial place for foreigners. That is why it has been called the Field of Blood to this day. Then what was spoken by Jeremiah the prophet was fulfilled: "They took the thirty pieces of silver, the price set on him by the people of Israel, and they used them to buy the potter's field, as the Lord commanded me."

Judas tried to return the money, a mere thirty pieces of silver, to his employer. He wanted to undo what was clearly set in motion, the execution of Christ. But the Pharisees were not interested in modifying their plans. The money was now sickening to Judas. He threw it all in the temple and promptly found a place to take his own life.

The Field of Blood represents a memorial to the horrible legacy of Judas and is a reminder of the words of Jesus in Matthew 6:24:

No one can serve two masters. Either he will hate the one and love the other or he will be devoted to one and despise the other. You cannot serve both God and money.

The contrasts used here are stark, black-and-white extremes. Love and hate cannot be comingled, nor can *devotion* and *despising*. Judas is Exhibit A of a case study about one who pretended to be devoted to God, but truly despised him. In the end, this misplaced love of money cost him everything.

HOW TO AVOID THE TRAP OF JOB SECURITY

Name the price that would cause you to become devoted to money. Have you ever thought about how much it would take? Thirty pieces of silver? Ten ounces of gold? Ten million dollars in the Mega Lottery? What if the price were much more subtle and disguised, like a substantial biweekly paycheck?

Often people sell out their devotion to Christ not for luxuries or riches, but for simple job security. Many will quietly sacrifice all of their time and energy in pursuit of financial security, while neglecting to allocate any time or energy to serving the One who provided the job.

Proverbs 30:7-9 expresses the appropriate heart attitude needed to truly trust God as our provider and to avoid the trap of putting our trust in our own efforts or in money:

> *Two things I ask of you, Lord; do not refuse me before I die:*
> *Keep falsehood and lies far from me; give me neither poverty*
> *nor riches, but give me only my daily bread. Otherwise, I*
> *may have too much and disown you and say, "Who is the*
> *Lord?" Or I may become poor and steal, and so dishonor the*
> *name of my God.*

Like Agur, who is attributed with these wise words, we must each walk in dependence upon God. It is he who provides our daily bread, and not us. God provides our needs through the work of our hands, but our hearts must remain fully reliant on him who gives us the ability to work. This heart attitude is expressed in the "Lord's Prayer" found in Matthew 6:11: *Give us today our daily bread.*

APPLICATION

Have you ever struggled with the tension between desiring job security and trusting God to provide for your needs?

Have you ever tried to serve two masters?

Do you long for more peace and less worry when it comes to your finances? If so, I suggest that you start by practicing these steps:

- Begin each day praying Proverbs 30:7-9.

- Work diligently in an area where God has gifted you.

- Thank God each day for his provision of your job, your income, and the things he has provided for you.

- Seek to increase your giving to God's work as he faithfully provides for your daily needs. This will break the temptation to grow dependent upon your income.

Demanding Money from God

Live the Great Commandment

LUKE 15:11-32

hristians know that the Parable of the Prodigal Son is a heart-rending story that demonstrates the radical love and grace of God. Yet, most of us fail to see that the story is replete with a series of financial mistakes that offer valuable lessons relevant to each of us.

In Luke 15, we read that the Pharisees muttered against Jesus as he ate with "sinners and tax collectors." Jesus addresses their self-righteousness by telling three parables. All have to do with the loss of monetary assets.

His first parable is about the shepherd who lost one sheep out of a flock of one hundred. "Why look for one sheep?" the Pharisees might have been thinking. "That's only a 1 percent loss. Looking for one sheep hardly seems worth the trouble." Of course, a sinner who realizes he needs a savior is very happy to know that God seeks even one lost sheep!

Jesus then raises the bar by telling a parable about the woman who lost one silver coin out of ten. A 10 percent loss is a significant amount of money, so the Pharisees no doubt perked up their ears at this parable. Their self-righteousness may have caused them to miss the main point, however, which is the good news that God searches for and redeems lost sinners.

Then Jesus increases the financial stakes by telling a story about a man who lost one of his two sons and, along with him, half of his property. This very familiar parable paints a poignant picture of the radical love of God in the face of man's rebellion and self-righteousness. Jesus began this way:

> *There was a man who had two sons. The younger one said to his father, "Father, give me my share of the estate." So he divided his property between them.* (v. 11-12)

How rude is that?! Jesus' audience must have been appalled. In the Jewish culture of that time, people didn't prepare estate plans and establish trusts to transfer assets in advance of death. Property simply passed to the heirs when its owner died. This brazen young man was essentially communicating to his dad, "I can't wait until you die. I want my money now." His unjustified demand is the height of presumption!

If you're a parent, how would you feel if your child said, "Give me my stuff! I don't care about you. I just want what you can give me!"

Have you ever said something like that to God? Do you sometimes think of him or talk with him as if he's a heavenly vending machine? When he doesn't give you what you want, do you get angry?

FAR TOO COMMON

A newspaper headline caught my eye on January 25, 2012. It read, "Pastor sentenced to prison for embezzling from church." Here's an excerpt from the sad story:

> United States Attorney Edward J. Tarver today announced the sentencing of 47-year-old Kenneth Terrell, former pastor of New Harvest International Ministries. In a six-hour sentencing hearing, attorneys presented evidence showing that Terrell had embezzled hundreds of thousands of dollars from the church over a span of at least four years while he was pastor.[1]

At a subconscious level, this former pastor probably presumed that he deserved more from God and the church. Perhaps he was even angry at God for not providing what he wanted when he wanted it. Regardless of what thoughts went through his mind, we can be sure that somehow he justified his decision to steal from God and his church.

A few preachers and evangelists embezzle in a much more subtle way. They teach their listeners to presume that God will give them whatever they desire. "Ask God for whatever you want," they proclaim, "and God is obligated to give it to you, if you have enough faith. It says so right in the Bible."

This is the "prosperity gospel," and it is an affront to God of the highest order. This lie has destroyed the lives and the faith of many who have heard it, along with the reputations and ministries of many who have preached it.

The prosperity gospel attracts big crowds and lots of money, because it's what "itching ears" want to hear. Those who preach that "God will give you what you want" are really more interested in getting what they want.

Consequences

Making demands on God or others can lead to big financial mistakes. In this parable, the prodigal's presumptive get-rich-quick scheme led to his utter devastation:

> *Not long after that, the younger son got together all he had, set off for a distant country and there squandered his wealth in wild living. After he had spent everything, there was a severe famine in that whole country, and he began to be in need. So he went and hired himself out to a citizen of that country, who sent him to his fields to feed pigs. He longed to fill his stomach with the pods that the pigs were eating, but no one gave him anything.* (v. 3-16)

These words would have shocked the Jewish audience. Jews were forbidden by God from eating pork. This prodigal not only would have eaten pork, he wished he could have eaten the slop that pigs ate. Along with his money, he had lost his dignity as the heir of a wealthy Hebrew family.

When we "love the bread, more than the Baker," our lives are on the sure path to moral and spiritual bankruptcy. We are truly rich when we have a loving relationship with God and mutually loving relationships in community with the people he places in our lives. When money takes the place of any of these relationships, we experience loneliness, misery, and despair. This was the prodigal's situation. He was truly poor. But there's more to the story:

> *When he came to his senses, he said, "How many of my father's hired servants have food to spare, and here I am starving to death! I will set out and go back to my father and say to him: Father, I have sinned against heaven and against you. I am no longer worthy to be called your son; make me like one of your hired servants." So he got up and went to his father.*

But while he was still a long way off, his father saw him and
was filled with compassion for him; he ran to his son, threw
his arms around him and kissed him. (v. 17-20)

Picture the scene as this once-rejected father joyfully hugs and kisses his pitiful, smelly, contrite son. We all are like the prodigal, because we all have grievously sinned against our Heavenly Father. But no matter how great our sins, God's mercy and grace are greater. From this parable we learn that nothing can separate us from the love of God. Nothing!

Like the prodigal in this parable, we can acknowledge our sins, repent, and return to the loving arms of our Father. God extends his grace to each of us, no matter how far we have strayed and no matter how horrible our financial mistakes.

HOW TO AVOID THE TRAP OF PRESUMPTION

When we presume that others should behave in a certain way, we place unjustified expectations on them and set ourselves up for disappointment. When things don't work out the way we desire, we get angry and judgmental and may attempt to take matters into our own hands. This type of presumption damages relationships, especially our relationship with God, and it opens the door to life-destroying frustrations and temptations.

When we presume that others will act in a certain way, we can get into serious trouble when things don't work out the way we expect. This is especially true when we have unrealistic expectations, demands, or presumptions of what, how, or when God will provide.

Presumption upon God to bail me out of a financial crisis or meet my hopes and dreams for a lifestyle that I expect is sending a message that I am more interested in the possessions than in my relationship with him.

Jesus said, *"No one can serve two masters. Either you will hate the one and love the other, or you will be devoted to the one and despise the other. You cannot serve both God and money."*

(Luke 16:13)

One sure way to avoid the tragic mistake of presumption is to practice the Great Commandment:

Love the Lord your God with all your heart and with all your soul and with all your strength and with all your mind, and Love your neighbor as yourself.

(Luke 10:27)

When we love God and our neighbors with all of our heart, we don't make demands of them to give us their material possessions. Love turns our attitude from what can they do to serve my needs, to what I can do to serve them.

---

[1]http://blog.congregationalsecurityinc.com/2012/01/pastor-sentenced-to-prison-for-embezzling-from-church/#.UYW7-MrwB8E

APPLICATION

Have you been captivated, either overtly or subtly, by the false prosperity gospel? Are you trying to serve two masters in any area of your life?

If you have made a terrible financial mistake, confess this to God and repent of your sin. Recognize his limitless love and mercy on each of us who have played the part of the prodigal son. He is ready to run to you and welcome you home.

Commit to serve God and not money by living the Great Commandment.

Identify your greatest financial concerns. Now, cast all of your worries, cares, and fears on the Lord. Trust him to provide for you as you faithfully serve those he has put in your life.

If you have never understood how to manage money God's way or have been involved in the false teaching of the prosperity gospel, I encourage you to go to *www.crown.org* and get involved in the *MoneyLife® Personal Finance Study*. This in depth course will help you understand much more on this vital topic.

chapter 16

Losing Your Soul

Never Compromise Your Integrity

Matthew 28:11-15

ow we use money reveals what we believe about money. Larry Burkett liked to say, "We each write our autobiography with our financial choices."

The Pharisees clearly viewed money as power. They thought their money had enough power to suppress the truth about the resurrection of Jesus Christ, the greatest event the world has ever known. It's remarkable that this deception, which may trump all other bad financial decisions in the Bible, gets so little notice.

On Resurrection Sunday, the men guarding the tomb rushed to their employers, the chief priests, to report that the body of Jesus had gone missing. This was not what the chief priests had expected or wanted to hear!

They used their money to protect their job security by having Jesus crucified. Now, their job security would be jeopardized even more if the public even thought that Jesus was alive. So, they sprang yet another despicable financial plan into action:

> *When the chief priests had met with the elders and devised*
> *a plan, they gave the soldiers a large sum of money, telling*
> *them, "You are to say, 'His disciples came during the night and*
> *stole him away while we were asleep.' If this report gets to the*
> *governor, we will satisfy him and keep you out of trouble."*
> (v. 12-14)

The Bible records that the elders joined the chief priests in this plan to bribe the guards. While we don't know how many were involved, we do know that they were able to come up with a "large sum of money." Money is no object when job security is at stake!

> *So the soldiers took the money and did as they were instructed.*
> *And this story has been widely circulated among the Jews to*
> *this very day.* (v. 15)

In agreeing to take this bribe, the soldiers cast this heretical lie into thousands of years of history.

LIES AND DAMNED LIES

Lies are evil. They bring destruction to both the perpetrators and the victims. Unfortunately, many people will readily lie for financial gain, with hardly a thought about the harmful consequences their deceptions have on others. This was the case with the guards mentioned above, and it sadly was the case in the following story.

On May 12, 2008, a great earthquake hit Sichuan, China, killing more than 69,000 people and injuring more than 300,000. A few of my friends were present to render aid just days after the disaster. They described horrific scenes of chaos and death, which to them seemed like a glimpse of hell. As people dug frantically through the rubble to rescue survivors, the agonizing cries of thousands of children could be heard coming from beneath collapsed school buildings.

It was widely known that the school buildings collapsed because they were not built to earthquake standards. The official report blamed "shoddy construction," but in truth the contractors had cut corners to increase their profits. A few well-placed bribes had kept the building inspectors away while they carried out their deception. The result: 5,335 children killed and 546 disabled.

Talk about losing souls for the sake of money! Yet, this doesn't compare to the destruction caused by the lie crafted by the Pharisees in an attempt to cover the truth of the resurrection of Jesus Christ.

CONSEQUENCES

Lies rob the liar of inner peace and harm those who are deceived. Ultimately, the corrosive power of lies hardens hearts and destroys souls. Imagine the deadened souls of the chief priests, the elders, and the guards who attempted one of the biggest deceptions in history.

Lies attempt to make good evil and evil good. They subvert the joy and liberty that comes from walking in the truth. A person, a family, a religion, a company, or a nation that accepts a culture of lying will ultimately suffer ruin.

How to Avoid the Trap of Losing Your Soul

Satan will use money to test our integrity in large and small ways. If he can gain a small victory, he will use that open door to offer larger opportunities to do his work. If a person is willing to tell a small lie for $1, how much more lying will he do for $1,000 or $1,000,000? We must learn to maintain a personal policy of not compromising our integrity.

A person of integrity is by definition a person whose character is "integrated, whole, undivided." The Bible is full of promises for those who practice absolute integrity:

> *Whoever of you loves life and desires to see many good days,*
> *keep your tongue from evil and your lips from telling lies.*
> *Turn from evil and do good; seek peace and pursue it.*
> (Psalm 34:12-14)

> *The greedy bring ruin to their households, but the one who*
> *hates bribes will live.*
> (Proverbs 15:27)

> *Do not pervert justice or show partiality. Do not accept a*
> *bribe, for a bribe blinds the eyes of the wise and twists the*
> *words of the innocent.*
> (Deuteronomy 16:19)

Cling to these promises instead of to money if you desire to enjoy a blessed life of peace filled with rich relationships with God, family, and friends.

APPLICATION

Whenever you are tempted to lie, cheat, accept a bribe, or hide the truth, remind yourself that God promises to provide for your every need. Even though truthfulness may cause you to lose something of temporal value, over the long run you will keep something of eternal value: your soul!

For inspiration and encouragement, remember this promise of God to those who operate with total integrity:

> *He who walks righteously and speaks what is right, who rejects gain from extortion and keeps his hand from accepting bribes, who stops his ears against plots of murder and shuts his eyes against contemplating evil – this is the man who will dwell on the heights, whose refuge will be the mountain fortress. His bread will be supplied, and water will not fail him.*
>
> (Isaiah 33:15-16)

To experience the benefits promised to a person of integrity, this verse makes it clear we must:

- Walk in the ways of righteousness (God's ways).
- Speak the truth.
- Reject any gain offered in exchange for a lie or deception.
- Turn away from considering, or even listening to, any evil deed.

chapter

Financial Hypocrisy

Crucify the Desires of the Flesh

ACTS 5:1-11

nanias and Sapphira made a terrible mistake in thinking they could cheat Christ's Church and get away with it. To appreciate the gravity of their mistake, it's helpful to understand the context in which it occurred. About fifty days after Jesus' resurrection, the early disciples experienced a remarkable event that is described in Acts 2:1-4:

When the day of Pentecost came, they were all together in one place. Suddenly a sound like the blowing of a violent wind came from heaven and filled the whole house where they were sitting. They saw what seemed to be tongues of fire that separated and came to rest on each of them. All of them were filled with the Holy Spirit and began to speak in other tongues as the Spirit enabled them.

After this empowering of the Holy Spirit, the disciples were on fire for God:

They devoted themselves to the apostles' teaching and to the fellowship, to the breaking of bread and to prayer. Everyone was filled with awe, and many wonders and miraculous signs were done by the apostles. All the believers were together and had everything in common. Selling goods, they gave to anyone as he had need.

Every day they continued to meet together in the temple courts. They broke bread in their homes and ate together with glad and sincere hearts, praising God and enjoying favor of all the people. And the Lord added to their number daily those who were being saved.

(Acts 2:42 – 47)

The early Christians cared for each other and for other people in pure and unselfish ways that evidenced the life-altering impact of the gospel. They didn't merely "talk the talk"; they "walked the walk."

All the believers were one in heart and mind. No one claimed that any of his possessions was his own. With great power the apostles continued to testify to the resurrection of the Lord Jesus, and much grace was upon them all. There were no needy persons among them. For from time to time those who owned lands or houses sold them, brought the money from the sales and put it at the apostles' feet, and it was distributed to anyone as he had need.

Joseph, a Levite from Cyprus, whom the apostles called Barnabas (which means Son of Encouragement), sold a field he owned and brought the money and put it at the apostles' feet.

What amazing generosity! No doubt, Barnabas created quite a stir. Perhaps that's why a husband and wife decided to imitate his actions, but with one difference:

Now a man named Ananias, together with his wife, Sapphira, also sold a piece of property. With his wife's full knowledge he kept back part of the money for himself, but brought the rest and put it at the apostles' feet. (v. 36-37)

Ananias and Sapphira appear to be united in heart and mind with the other believers, but by secretly holding back from the Lord, they are committing the sin of hypocrisy. A bit later, we'll get to the rest of their story.

FINANCIAL HYPOCRITES

Millions of people on both ends of the financial spectrum commit the sin of financial hypocrisy every day. Proverbs 13:7 tells us two ways:

One person pretends to be rich, yet has nothing; another pretends to be poor, yet has great wealth.

Jesus severely rebuked the financial hypocrites who cultivated the external appearance of generosity but refused to deal with the internal issues of greed, self-righteousness, and hardheartedness.

Woe to you, teachers of the law and Pharisees, you hypocrites! You clean the outside of the cup and dish, but inside they are full of greed and self-indulgence.

(Matthew 23:25)

Woe to you Pharisees, because you give God a tenth of your mint, rue and all other kinds of garden herbs, but you neglect justice and the love of God. You should have practiced the latter without leaving the former undone.

(Luke 12:42)

Sometimes financial hypocrisy is easy to spot. Imelda Marcos, a politician and the widow of former Philippine President Ferdinand Marcos, once owned 2,700 pairs of ladies shoes. She famously defended her extravagant lifestyle by saying it was her duty to be "some kind of light, a star to give [the poor] guidelines."

At other times, financial hypocrisy is more subtle, especially when it occurs within the church. The late Oral Roberts made national headlines when appealing for financial support to build Oral Roberts University. During a fundraising drive in January 1987, Roberts announced to a television audience that unless he raised $8 million by that March, God would "call him home." In effect, he was telling his listeners that if they didn't donate generously enough, God would punish them by taking away their pastor.

CONSEQUENCES

Getting back to our story of Ananias and Sapphira, in Acts 5:3-5 we read about how the Apostle Peter confronted Ananias:

Then Peter said, "Ananias, how is it that Satan has so filled your heart that you have lied to the Holy Spirit and have kept for yourself some of the money you received for the land? Didn't it belong to you before it was sold? And after it was sold, wasn't the money at your disposal? What made you think of doing such a thing? You have not lied to men, but to God."

*When Ananias heard this, he fell down and died. And great
fear seized all who heard what had happened. Then some
young men came forward, wrapped up his body, and carried
him out and buried him.*

God does not tolerate financial hypocrisy! Peter subsequently confronted
Sapphira about her part in this deception, and she also suffered a sudden
death.

The exact cause of their deaths is unclear, but the reason for them is very
clear. This incident is a stark warning that we should never attempt to
deceive God or his Church. I believe the severity of penalty for this couple
indicates how serious God regards this sin. Jesus wants a Church that puts
his words into action.

"Inconsistency on the part of pastors and the faithful between what they
say and what they do, between word and manner of life, is undermining
the Church's credibility," Pope Francis recently said in his homily. He was
being kind and gentle.

Acts 8:9-25 introduces us to Simon the Sorcerer, a man who had a significant
reputation within his community because of his magical powers. When he
saw the power of the Holy Spirit manifested through the Apostle Peter,
he offered to pay Peter money to acquire some of that same power. Notice
how sternly Peter rebukes him:

*Peter answered: "May your money perish with you, because
you thought you could buy the gift of God with money! You
have no part or share in this ministry, because your heart
is not right before God. Repent of this wickedness and pray
to the Lord in the hope that he may forgive you for having
such a thought in your heart. For I see that you are full of
bitterness and captive to sin.* (v. 20-23)

How to Avoid the Trap of Financial Hypocrisy

To avoid the serious sins of greed and financial hypocrisy, we must voluntarily die to our personal desires.

> *Those who belong to Christ Jesus have crucified the flesh*
> *with its passions and desires. Since we live by the Spirit, let*
> *us keep in step with the Spirit. Let us not become conceited,*
> *provoking and envying each other.*
> (Galatians 5:24-26)

Death by crucifixion is slow and painful. But for the Christian, it's followed by a splendid new birth. Permit me to tell you a personal story.

For years, I wanted to be rich. I reasoned that being a rich Christian was far better than being a poor Christian. On the outside I looked like a devoted follower of Christ, but inwardly I was obsessed with money and wanted to get as much of it as possible. I hated sermons on giving and tithing, but I loved the ones on getting and receiving!

Not until I experienced a painful setback in business did I realize what a hypocritical, double-minded man I truly was. Once convicted of this sin, with the help of the Holy Spirit I crucified my passion to get rich. The death was agonizing, but almost instantly I came alive to the excitement and joy of giving myself fully to God's purposes and not my own.

APPLICATION

- Make a list of any areas where you have been a financial hypocrite.

- Ask the Lord to reveal the root of your desires and passions, so that you can experience a spiritual death to the flesh.

- Turn from those desires by confessing them to God. Ask him to make your heart pure.

- Keep in step with the Holy Spirit, who will teach you to speak and act in accordance with the truth.

- Make all financial decisions with the desire to please God as your foremost goal.

Exchanging True Riches for Faux Riches

Seek First the Kingdom of God

Revelation 3:14-22

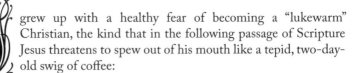 grew up with a healthy fear of becoming a "lukewarm" Christian, the kind that in the following passage of Scripture Jesus threatens to spew out of his mouth like a tepid, two-day-old swig of coffee:

These are the words of the Amen, the faithful and true witness, the ruler of God's creation. I know your deeds, that you are neither cold nor hot. I wish you were either one or the other! So, because you are lukewarm—neither hot nor cold—I am about to spit you out of my mouth. You say, 'I am rich; I have acquired wealth and do not need a thing.'

(Revelation 3:14-17)

This led me to do my best at attending church, attempting some guilt-driven evangelism, and striving to be a good person in the eyes of God. But when I became an adult and studied this passage more carefully, I was surprised to notice that it was about money! This letter was written to caution to the church of Laodicea against committing a massive financial blunder. Let's take a closer look at their very real issue.

This congregation's root problem is money. It's not a mistake to have money, but having money has led them to a false conclusion. They have concluded that because they have such great wealth, they don't need anything... including God! Money has become their source for success, security, and significance. They have replaced their Savior with their savings.

Because of their independent attitude, these people have lost their unique identification as the people of God. God is essentially telling them that they are operating at "room temperature." They are not colder than the culture, and they are not hotter than the culture. They have simply blended in with the world and become completely indistinguishable from it. Having become like the world in their reliance upon wealth, they are now unsuitable for fulfilling God's purposes.

WORTHLESS

In November 2008, due to a disastrous economic policy and other factors, the rate of inflation in Zimbabwe reached an estimated sextillion percent (that's a ten with twenty-one zeros after it!). At one point the government printed a $100 Trillion Zim Dollar bill. That is $100,000,000,000,000. With that bill, a person could buy an inexpensive lunch, but no soda to go with it. The money was not worth the paper it was being printed on.

Imagine if during that period of hyperinflation you saw a citizen of Zimbabwe hold up one of those bills and shout, *"I am rich! I have $100 trillion Zim Dollars! I have acquired wealth and do not need a thing."* You'd probably think he was crazy. That's exactly how ridiculous the church of Laodicea must have sounded to the ears of God.

I own one of those $100 Trillion Zim Dollar bills. I keep it in my Bible to remind me that being rich in man's economy and being rich in God's economy are truly incomparable.

THE CONSEQUENCES OF THINKING WE ARE RICH

"The silver is mine and the gold is mine,"
declares the Lord Almighty.
(Haggai 2:8)

How would you like to own all the silver and gold in the world? God already does, and that's just the beginning. He also owns all of the other assets and "unsearchable riches" that exist in this vast universe that he created.

No man is truly rich apart from Christ. The annual "Forbes Richest List" should be renamed the "Faux Riches List." It is a great delusion to think that holding a billion dollars of worldly treasures qualifies a man to be "rich." In comparison to God, every man is a pauper, regardless of the amount of money and assets he has temporarily accumulated.

The pursuit of riches, comfort, and pleasure has stirred the imaginations and fueled the desires of men and women since the beginning of time. Some have been extraordinarily successful at this pursuit, while others have wasted most of their life energy chasing after "just a little bit more."

Both types of people commit a terrible financial mistake. But perhaps the greatest tragedy is suffered by those who are so successful at gaining the faux riches of the world that they completely miss the "true riches" found only in a vibrant relationship with Jesus Christ.

How to Avoid Exchanging True Riches for Worldly Riches

I have heard it said that all a person really needs for happiness in life is something to become passionate about. This is not true. While passion does enrich our life journey with excitement and colorful experiences, we can become passionate about the wrong things. God wants us to be passionate about serving him and expanding his kingdom, not about trying to fill a temporary bucket with worldly riches and pleasures. In the end, the bucket will be filled with nothing more than Zim dollars.

In Matthew 6, Jesus was speaking to another group of folks who were definitely not wealthy. In fact, they were probably under severe financial stress, because they asked him questions like, "What shall we eat? What shall we drink? What shall we wear?" As a friend of mine from Kentucky is fond of saying, "These are not high-class problems; these are the basic necessities."

Jesus' response may at first seem a bit insensitive and idealistic for such real, immediate, and painful needs. He said:

> *And why do you worry about clothes? See how the flowers*
> *of the field grow. They do not labor or spin. Yet I tell you*
> *that not even Solomon in all his splendor was dressed like*
> *one of these. If that is how God clothes the grass of the field,*
> *which is here today and tomorrow is thrown into the fire,*
> *will he not much more clothe you—you of little faith? So do*
> *not worry, saying, "What shall we eat'" or "What shall we*
> *drink?" or "What shall we wear?"* (v. 28-31)

Many in the crowd probably thought, "Is that the best Jesus can do? Is he simply going to tell us not to worry? Is he that naive?" But Jesus didn't stop there. He went on to offer the most remarkable and profound financial advice the world has ever known:

> *For the pagans run after all these things, and your heavenly*
> *Father knows that you need them. But seek first his kingdom*
> *and his righteousness, and all these things will be given to*
> *you as well. Therefore do not worry about tomorrow, for*
> *tomorrow will worry about itself. Each day has enough*
> *trouble of its own.* (v. 32-34)

So, Jesus says, if you want to stop worrying about your financial needs, stop running after your "thingdom." Seek first the kingdom of God and his righteousness, and make God the chief object and aim of your desires. Put everything else in second place.

Notice how well this aligns with the advice given to the church at Laodicea, which thought it had no needs. Here's the rest of that conversation:

> *But you do not realize that you are wretched, pitiful, poor,*
> *blind and naked. I counsel you to buy from me gold refined in*
> *the fire, so you can become rich; and white clothes to wear, so*
> *you can cover your shameful nakedness; and salve to*
> *put on your eyes, so you can see.*
> (Revelation 3:17-18)

Over and over again, the Bible tells us to stop relying on worldly wealth and seek the riches of Christ. Quit chasing after faux riches and pursue true riches. But gaining true riches is a costly business, as these words of Jesus make clear:

> *Then he said to them all: "Whoever wants to be my disciple*
> *must deny themselves and take up their cross daily and follow*
> *me. For whoever wants to save their life will lose it, but*
> *whoever loses their life for me will save it."*
> (Luke 9:23-24)

Does this mean we are to stop working and simply live "by faith"? Of course not! God designed us to work, and we should use the skills and resources he has given us to provide for our needs.

But God doesn't want us to place our faith in the world's wealth. As we work, we place our hope and faith in him, not in our job, our talents, or our bank account. This is the path to true discipleship and lasting joy. Whether we have much worldly wealth or little, we can all overflow with the true riches promised to those who are faithful to God.

APPLICATION

Use the following three-step plan to put these principles into practice:

Make a Balance Sheet.

- On the left side, in a column titled "Worldly Riches," list all of your worldly assets: your money, real estate, cars, stocks, bonds, and personal possessions that you have accumulated by the work of your hands.

- On the right side, in a column titled "True Riches," list the riches that have been provided by the grace and goodness of God: your personal salvation; your relationships with God, your spouse, your children, your extended family, your church, and your friends; your health; your five senses; answered prayers; and anything else you can think of that has blessed your life.

Make a Decision.

Evaluate what you would exchange from the column on the right side (True Riches) for more of the column on the left side (Worldly Riches).

If you are like most people, you would not forfeit any of your true riches for more worldly riches. Your salvation, your family, and your relationships are of far greater value than anything else in your life.

Create a Strategy.

Create a strategy to gain more true riches and to help lead others to make a similar exchange. This may include daily Bible study, more active participation and leadership in your home and church, leading others through this material in a small group study, or reaching out to your community to meet local needs.

The opportunities are endless. They will become even more apparent once you make the decision to become intentional about this exchange.

Avoid the financial mistake of the Laodiceans and buy the gold that God himself has refined in the fire. It will be the greatest financial decision you will ever make.

Foolish Procrastination

Invest Now for Christ's Return

Matthew 25:1-13

he fascinating Parable of the Ten Virgins contains a serious financial mistake made by 50% of the people in the story. We need to examine it closely.

This story is told in response to the disciples' original question to Jesus in Matthew 24:3.

As Jesus was sitting on the Mount of Olives, the disciples came to him privately. "Tell us," they said, "when will this happen, and what will be the sign of your coming and of the end of the age?"

Jesus had already given them a list of signs and warnings regarding the end of the age as well as a clear reminder that no man knows the real hour but all should be ready. To punctuate the urgency of this call to be ready, he tells the poignant story of what the kingdom of God will be like. I want you to read the entire account in Matthew 25 before we go through some of the specific lessons from this parable.

At that time the kingdom of heaven will be like ten virgins who took their lamps and went out to meet the bridegroom. Five of them were foolish and five were wise. The foolish ones took their lamps but did not take any oil with them. The wise ones, however, took oil in jars along with their lamps. The bridegroom was a long time in coming, and they all became drowsy and fell asleep.

"At midnight the cry rang out: 'Here's the bridegroom! Come out to meet him!'

"Then all the virgins woke up and trimmed their lamps. The foolish ones said to the wise, 'Give us some of your oil; our lamps are going out.'

"'No,' they replied, 'there may not be enough for both us and you. Instead, go to those who sell oil and buy some for yourselves.'

But while they were on their way to buy the oil, the bridegroom arrived. The virgins who were ready went in with him to the wedding banquet. And the door was shut.

"Later the others also came. 'Lord, Lord,' they said, 'open the door for us!'

"But he replied, 'Truly I tell you, I don't know you.'

"Therefore keep watch, because you do not know the day or the hour."

COMMON DENOMINATORS OF THE TEN VIRGINS

- All are virgins.

- All have been waiting for the same event, the wedding banquet of the bridegroom.

- All have lamps.

- All fell asleep waiting for the bridegroom's return.

- All wake up at midnight when the cry rang out that the bridegroom was coming.

- All had the money and access to oil to have obtained extra for their lamps.

- All needed their lamp and oil to get to the wedding banquet.

THE GREAT DIVIDE BETWEEN THE TEN VIRGINS

The Five Foolish Women

- Had lamps but no oil.

- Had not purchased oil in preparation for the event.

- Asked the five wise women for their oil but did not receive any.

- Had to leave the group in procession to the wedding banquet.

- Had to purchase oil after the bridegroom was on his way.

- Missed the event entirely.

- Were not recognized by the bridegroom when they arrived late to the banquet.

The Five Wise Women

- Had lamps and oil.

- Purchased the oil in preparation for the coming event.

- Did not have oil they were able to give to the five foolish women.

- Had enough oil to complete the journey.

- Were recognized by the bridegroom.

The clear point of the story: do not be foolish and procrastinate, get ready now for the return of Christ!

PROCRASTINATORS

Even though we know that Christmas comes on time every year on December 25th, retail stores are crammed with shoppers picking up last minute gifts in the final hours of December 24th.

Even though we know a car must have gasoline to operate properly, we still run out of gas! Has that ever happened to anybody you know?

Even though we know our income taxes are due April 15th of every year, about 40% of taxpayers wait until the final weeks, days and hours to file their federal returns.

Even though we know that Christ will return as he promised, we postpone getting serious about our total commitment to his kingdom.

CONSEQUENCES

Procrastination is a part of human nature. Those who are foolish develop a habit of postponing matters that are not deemed urgent. With all good intentions, they run the risk of waiting until it is too late. When the car loses power and begins to coast to a full stop before you can arrive at your destination, it is too late.

The foolish women had every intention of attending the wedding banquet and appeared committed in many ways, but they failed to exchange the money in their pocket for the oil that was needed. The cost was enormous. First, they were late to the event and missed the banquet altogether. But more importantly, when they finally purchased the oil, the door was closed to the banquet and the bridegroom responded with these piercing words, "I don't know you." This was spoken to the very ones who referred to the bridegroom as their *Lord*.

HOW TO AVOID THE TRAP OF FOOLISH PROCRASTINATION

Many in the world consider themselves to be very religious. Many have great respect and admiration for Jesus Christ. Many refer to him as a great prophet. Many are eager for him to return and bring peace to a fallen world. But many will hear, "I don't know you" if they have not been born again by the Spirit.

Paul expresses this same urgent concern in 2 Corinthians 13:5:

> *Put yourselves to the test to see if you are in the faith;*
> *examine yourselves! Or do you not recognize regarding*
> *yourselves that Jesus Christ is in you unless, indeed, you fail*
> *the test!*

It is an assumption, but likely a valid one, that Jesus was sharing this story as an allegory that points out that the missing "oil in the lamps" of the ten virgins can be compared to a very religious person who is missing the redemption of Jesus Christ.

chapter 19

APPLICATION

Now that you know some of the worst financial mistakes in the Bible, don't procrastinate from putting oil in your lamp. The good news is that this oil cannot be purchased but is a free gift from God found in Christ Jesus.

Romans 6:23

For the wages of sin is death, but the gift of God is eternal life in Christ Jesus our Lord.

Romans 10:9-11

If you declare with your mouth, "Jesus is Lord," and believe in your heart that God raised him from the dead, you will be saved. For it is with your heart that you believe and are justified, and it is with your mouth that you profess your faith and are saved. As Scripture says, "Anyone who believes in him will never be put to shame."

Crown has produced an excellent short film titled, "Lifted Up" in the *God Provides*® series. It is a powerful teaching tool about a personal relationship with Christ or for witnessing to others.

If you have found a renewed relationship with Jesus Christ through this book, please write us and share your testimony with us. You can find our address at **www.crown.org**.

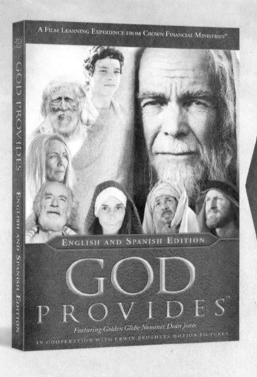

Overcoming Financial Challenges To Help You Achieve a Life of Meaning and Purpose

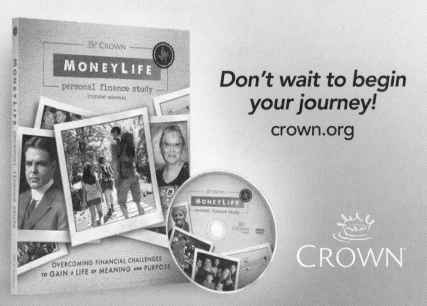

Don't wait to begin your journey!
crown.org

Unlock Your Potential.
Do More. Be More.

Career Direct® is a unique assessment and consultation program designed to help you maximize your God-given talents and abilities. Unlocking the full picture of your design with a trained, godly Career Direct Consultant makes the process easy and exciting.

God has created you with a specific combination of Personality, Interests, Skills, and Values. We're excited to help you in discovering how you're wired and give you more confidence in making occupational and educational choices.

Visit **www.careerdirect.org** to get connected to a trained Career Direct Consultant.

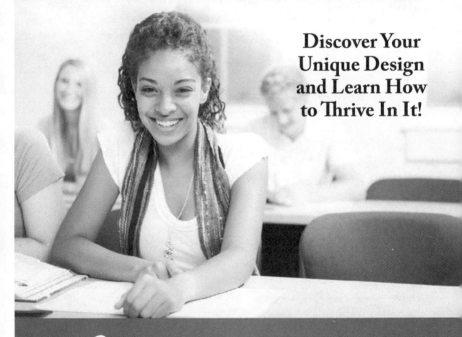

Discover Your Unique Design and Learn How to Thrive In It!